For Anne & Leela

Contents

New Poems

from
A Generation of Peace

Dancing

Having been where contrasts meet,
I perceive reality to be
whatever looms largest in the mind.

Thus, truths are never absolute;
nebulous, they never lose the shifting
beat of music changing time.

Books I read, and faces seen
in sunlight tell me where I am;
at night, this truth melts away;

an older truth looms within
and I submit, take my rifle,
rejoin comrades on patrol

until the sun returns the books,
and faces, and the other truth
I dance with to a kinder beat.

The Next Step

The next step you take
may lead you into an ambush.

The next step you take
may trigger a tripwire.

The next step you take
may detonate a mine.

The next step you take
may tear your leg off at the hip.

The next step you take
may split your belly open.

The next step you take
may send a sniper's bullet through your brain.

The next step you take.
The next step you take.

The next step.
The next step.

The next step.

Guerrilla War

It's practically impossible
to tell civilians
from the Viet Cong.

Nobody wears uniforms.
They all talk
the same language
(and you couldn't understand them
even if they didn't).

They tape grenades
inside their clothes,
and carry satchel charges
in their market baskets.

Even their women fight.
And young boys.
And girls.

It's practically impossible
to tell civilians
from the Viet Cong.

After awhile,
you quit trying.

Souvenirs

"Bring me back a souvenir," the captain called.
"Sure thing," I shouted back above the amtrac's roar.

Later that day,
the column halted,
we found a Buddhist temple by the trail.
Combing through a nearby wood,
we found a heavy log as well.

It must have taken more than half an hour,
but at last we battered in
the concrete walls so badly
that the roof collapsed.

Before it did,
I took two painted vases
Buddhists use for burning incense.

One vase I kept,
and one I offered proudly to the captain.

Hunting

Sighting down the long black barrel,
I wait till front and rear sights
form a perfect line on his body,
then slowly squeeze the trigger.

The thought occurs
that I have never hunted anything in my whole life
except other men.

But I have learned by now
where such thoughts lead,
and soon pass on
to chow, and sleep,
and how much longer till I change my socks.

The Bob Hope Christmas Special

They went to Cam Ranh Bay,
to Saigon, and Danang—
to anywhere that was secure,
that had good roads, and showers.

They made the headlines
with their bombshell girls
and dedication to the boys.

They never got to where the fighting was,
to where the face of yesterday
looked exactly like today.

They never gave a show for those
who found relief in cigarettes,
dry socks, and no patrol today.

In thirteen months,
I never saw the USO.
But once in August, near Hoi An,
Floyd Patterson shook my hand.

A Relative Thing

We are the ones you sent to fight a war
you didn't know a thing about.

It didn't take us long to realize
the only land that we controlled
was covered by the bottoms of our boots.

When the newsmen said that naval ships
had shelled a VC staging point,
we saw a breastless woman
and her stillborn child.

We laughed at old men stumbling
in the dust in frenzied terror
to avoid our three-ton trucks.

We fought outnumbered in Hue City
while the ARVN soldiers looted bodies
in the safety of the rear.
The cookies from the wives of Local 104
did not soften our awareness.

We have seen the pacified supporters
of the Saigon government
sitting in their jampacked cardboard towns,
their wasted hands placed limply in their laps,
their empty bellies waiting for the rice
some district chief has sold
for profit to the Viet Cong.

We have been Democracy on Zippo raids,

burning houses to the ground,
driving eager amtracs through new-sown fields.

We are the ones who have to live
with the memory that we were the instruments
of your pigeon-breasted fantasies.
We are inextricable accomplices
in this travesty of dreams:
but we are not alone.

We are the ones you sent to fight a war
you did not know a thing about—
those of us that lived
have tried to tell you what went wrong.
Now you think you do not have to listen.

Just because we will not fit
into the uniforms of photographs
of you at twenty-one
does not mean you can disown us.

We are your sons, America,
and you cannot change that.
When you awake,
we will still be here.

Imagine

The conversation turned to Vietnam.
He'd been there, and they asked him
what it had been like:
had he been in battle?
Had he ever been afraid?

Patiently, he tried to answer
questions he had tried to answer
many times before.

They listened, and they strained
to visualize the words:
newsreels and photographs, books
and Wilfred Owen tumbled
through their minds.
Pulses quickened.

They didn't notice, as he talked,
his eyes, as he talked,
his eyes begin to focus
through the wall, at nothing,
or at something inside.

When he finished speaking,
someone asked him:
had he ever killed?

from
A Generation of Peace
(Revised)

Making the Children Behave

Do they think of me now
in those strange Asian villages
where nothing ever seemed
quite human
but myself
and my few grim friends
moving through them
hunched
in lines?

When they tell stories to their children
of the evil
that awaits misbehavior,
is it me they conjure?

To Maynard on the Long Road Home

Biking at night with no lights
and no helmet, you were struck
and hurled sixty feet,
dead on impact.
The newspapers noted the irony:
surviving the war
to die like that, alone,
on a hometown street.
I knew better.

Years before, on Christmas Day,
I met you on a road near Quang Tri,
a chance reunion of Perkasie boys
grown up together in a town
that feared God and raised sons
willing to die for their country.
"Who're you with?
Have you seen much action?
What the hell's going on here?"
All afternoon we remembered
our shared youth: the old boat
with Jeffy and the slow leak,
skipping Sunday School to read comics
and drink orange soda at Flexer's,
the covered bridge near Bryan's farm.
Though neither of us
spoke of it, we knew then
we had lost
more than our youth.

16

I show my poems to friends now and then,
hoping one or two might see
my idealistic bombast
in a new light:
the sharp turns of mood, anger
defying visible foundation,
inexplicable sadness.
How often they wonder aloud
how I managed to survive—
they always assume the war is over,
not daring to imagine our wounds,
or theirs, if it is not.
I think of you,
and wonder if either of us
will ever come home.

from
Rootless

The Flying Gypsy

I. Windward

She sits each night near Market Street.
And every night she wears the same
old dress and faded flowered hat
that must have fired young men's dreams
fifty years ago.
A battered Gimbel's shopping bag
holds everything she owns.

II. Leeward

Once, many years ago, I came
by chance upon a clipper ship
tied up beside an unused dock.
The Flying Gypsy was her name,
and in her time, white canvas bent
before the wind, she must have been
the swiftest lady on the sea,
for even then her rotting shrouds
and broken spars stretched anxious
fingers to the gentlest breeze.

III. Windward

I pass that way each night at ten.
No matter that I know by now,
before I see her, she'll be there;
in the quiet, empty street
her solitary presence always startles:
saying nothing, she demands her place
with eyes that stare through pounding waves
and lips still tasting salt.

21

Geese

When you went away,
the leaves began to fall;
the blue sky scattered before clouds
like flustered pigeons in the plaza,
and the geese by the river,
thinking winter had come,
cried out and fled.

All that day the colors
slowly drained from the world
like sand slipping through small
invisible holes in the earth.
The people lost their faces,
appearing only as bland shapes
at the ends of long tunnels.

Back home I discovered
a new silence
clinging to the walls like frost.
Later the wind came around to the north,
beating at the windows,
writing your name on the rattling glass,
and I could not sleep.

All this was a long time ago,
but the wind still blows from the north
and the frost on the walls remains.
The colors have not returned, nor the leaves
nor the faces nor the blue sky.
And I do not wonder any longer
when they will;
I only wonder how the geese knew.

Money in the Bank

for Alfred Starr Hamilton

Sixty-one years
of your life are gone and I
have never heard of you
until today.

I understand the poems
simply grow
beneath your pillow as you sleep
in your cheap boardinghouse room,
and you only have to rise
and type them in the morning,
ten at a crack before lunch
and the daily paper you read
at the Montclair Public Library
because you cannot afford your own,
like the cigarettes
you pick up from the street.

Sixty-one years old,
and I have never heard of you
because you are not taught in school
and your poems do not appear in *Poetry*
and your only book was not reviewed
because we have no use for poets
who have no use
for us.

Well, Mr. Hamilton,
now I have heard of you,
and tomorrow the mailman

will give you this
(along perhaps with another summons
from the Garden State
because they say you are a vagrant),
and you'll open it and find
some person that you do not know
has sent you money.

I'd like to say I sent you this
because I simply care
about another human being.

But the truth is, Mr. Hamilton,
this money you receive
is for myself,
and for the future,

and I send it out of fear.

To Those Who Have Gone Home Tired

After the streets fall silent
After the bruises and the tear-gassed eyes are healed
After the concensus has returned
After the memories of Kent and My Lai and Hiroshima
lose their power
and their connections with each other
and the sweaters labeled Made in Taiwan
After the last American dies in Canada
and the last Korean in prison
and the last Indian at Pine Ridge
After the last whale is emptied from the sea
and the last leopard emptied from its skin
and the last drop of blood refined by Exxon
After the last iron door clangs shut
behind the last conscience
and the last loaf of bread is hammered into bullets
and the bullets
scattered among the hungry

What answers will you find
What armor will protect you
when your children ask you

Why?

Going Home with the Monkeys

Another day gone;
we go home in winter twilight,
warm in our scarves and mufflers,
counting our small accomplishments
like fingers on a hand.

We did our jobs;
we were kind—
or if we were not,
tomorrow we can mend it.

It is evening;
we could rest—
except for the beggar on the corner,
a headline, a siren, a dream
of green palms in moonlight:

they rise up before us like wind,
like warnings,
and go away,
and rise up farther on.

They are the shadows of everything
except what we are
and what we have done.

And they never seem to get
any closer.

And they never leave us alone.

from
Empire

Letter

to a North Vietnamese soldier
whose life crossed paths with mine
in Hue City, February 5th, 1968

Thought you killed me
with that rocket? Well, you nearly did:
splattered walls and splintered air,
knocked me cold and full of holes,
and brought the roof down on my head.

But I lived,
long enough to wonder often
how you missed, long enough
to wish too many times
you hadn't.

What's it like back there?
It's all behind us here,
and after all those years of possibility,
things are back to normal.
We just had a special birthday,
and we've found again our inspiration
by recalling where we came from
and forgetting where we've been.

Oh, we're still haggling over pieces
of the lives sticking out
beyond the margins of our latest
history books—but no one haggles
with the authors.

    Do better than that
you cockeyed gunner with the brass

to send me back alive among a people
I can never feel
at ease with anymore:

remember where you've been, and why.
And then build houses; build villages,
dikes and schools, songs
and children in that green land
I blackened with my shadow
and the shadow of my flag.

Remember Ho Chi Minh
was a poet: please,
do not let it all come down
to nothing.

After the Fire

After the fire
burns out,
and the stillness
sweeps in, we
begin to observe
small things: red
welts, slight
bruises on
pubic bones, musky
impatience of wet lace—Oh, my
face in your
breasts, and
yours in my
hair, and the
laughter
softly lapping the night
like a sea.

Twodot, Montana

I knew that Sunday morning
only what I could see: dust
dancing in waves on a single unpaved street,
swirling in tiny plumes, unswirling,
blowing away through summer heat; two cats
asleep on a windowledge; a dog asleep
on the shade of the plank sidewalk;
squat frame buildings, half of them boarded shut.
I had followed Mac's directions perfectly;
this had to be Twodot—but I was lost.
Out of the car, I gingerly looked in windows:
peer in the barbershop-post office—nobody there;
peer in the Twodot Bar, where Saturday nights
the cowhands wash down whole weeks
of prairie dust-nobody there either.
At one end of town, the railroad station seemed
to collapse board by board as I watched, the train
coming once a year, loading cattle for slaughter.
Beyond the last buildings, a few small silver
Airstream Specials crouched, bolted to concrete
foundations against Canadian winter winds,
space between them for kitchen gardens.
A woman there answered my question:
on down the road ten more miles; Mary and Pete's
would be the Big House, the first one; the 'boy,'
Mac, lived in the Little House beyond that.
Clawing dry earth with a hoe as she talked, hair
stiff and pale as dry prairie grass, her eyes
fell back inside themselves like old volcanoes
or the insides of empty whiskey bottles,

something deep within resenting the intrusion
of people who come and go when they please.
I got in the car and left, thinking that morning,
"Perhaps because it's Sunday."

Welcome

When you have ridden once too often
jostling on the El
in a crowd at dusk with no one
to talk to and no one
waiting at home,

when you have eaten your last meal
alone,

when you have said your final
hello to the grocer
in that same strange voice
like a cry,

when you have given up hope
ever of turning the next corner
to find the door
with no lock and a lamp
burning on the other side,

you will come to the door
with no lock
and no lamp,

and you will open it.

Come in;
sit down, rest, and eat.
See: we have saved you a place
at our table.

Empire

I. Barbarian tribesmen
    stand in the light
    still on the crests of the hills.
    They shake their weapons in the air,
    gesture lewdly, and jeer
    at the soldiers in the valley
    where the watchfires
    flicker at the rising shadows.

    Down below, Roman officers
    drink wine and plan;
    soldiers tug cloaks
    more tightly around their shoulders,
    mutter about the food,
    and think of wives and lovers
    as the sentries take their posts
    around the camp: a circle of eyes
    peering into the darkness
    at the edge of the empire.

II. In Perkasie and Pittsburgh,
    North Platte, Grosse Point and Portland,
    Memorial Day crowds line the streets
    cheering for the local high school band.
    The majorettes are beautiful
    and young,
    and the solemn Legionnaires, young
    thirty years ago, fire
    fake bullets for the dead.
    Picnics follow in the afternoon,

and all across America
swimming pools open for the summer.

The honored dead are white,
or died
trying to be white,
red and blue: there are
no twenty-one gun salutes
for Crazy Horse.

On this day, in 1431,
Joan of Arc was burned to death
by the English
and the Catholic Church.
She died for France.

III. When the dinosaurs died,
     dim-witted and without complaint,
     they left behind
     a noble silence,
     and a world
     still capable of life.

IV. The great auks
    and the passenger pigeons
    are gone forever;
    the gorillas are in Lincoln Park Zoo.
    The redwood trees, poking
    into the clouds already when Christ
    calmed the turbulent waters of Galilee,
    are picket fences in Daly City.
    The whales—greys and blues, fins,
    humps and pilots—breaching for air, find
    only the patient harpooners' exploding barbs
    while the whooping cranes sail south
    each year in smaller numbers,

36

their nesting grounds
along the Texas Gulf of Mexico
cities now, and refineries.
The bald eagles die
unhatched in their eggs;
the dolphins die in the tunamen's nets.

V. Toward the end, they understood
it was no use
complaining: they began to pray,
truly believing their prayers
and in the God they prayed to,
calling each other
sister and brother, sharing
what food and shelter they could find.

In the darkness when they died,
they were alone.

The Spiders' White Dream of Peace

I've had nightmares before—this
wasn't an ordinary
nightmare that jerks you awake
at the last second, startled
but free—this was something else:
it was spiders telling their
secrets in my ear, at night,
alone with them in my bed—
I wasn't even asleep.
There were hundreds of them, all
crowding around me, crawling
on top of one another,
each trying to be the one—
be the first one—to tell me
their whole plan. It was easy
to see they wanted to please
me; I couldn't understand
why. They knew what we needed—
I couldn't believe it—I
tried to wake up; I couldn't.
They were plotting the end of
the world: together they would
rise up, rise as one army
of weavers, together spin
their delicate webs back and
forth, under and over, wrap
the whole earth in a cocoon
and leave it hanging in space—
a soft white ball forever
silent, preserved, without want.

An Exorcism

"If you're a writer, you should get up every morning
and give thanks that America is totally crazy."
—Michael Anania

Suddenly the woman fell down,
thrashing all around the floor
of the crowded lounge, screaming
"I've got seven devils in me!"
Not six, not eight—"Seven devils!"—
little red ones, with pitchforks.

"Whadaya expect us to do about it?"
said the paramedics to no one in particular,
scratching their heads,
fondling their fancy equipment.
The woman went on thrashing:
"I've got seven devils in me!"

"Call a priest," someone said; someone did.
"Oh seven devils," the priest intoned,
"in the name of the Lord, get out!
In the name of God,
by the body and blood of Christ,
oh seven devils, out! Out, out!"

It worked: "Ah!"
The woman stopped thrashing.
She wiped the foam from her bleeding lips,
stood up sheepishly, straightened her dress.
"Thank you, Father," she said;
"Oh thank you, Jesus, thank you.
America, thank you, thank you—
it's a blessing to be free."

A Confirmation

for Gerry Gaffney

Solemn Douglas firs stride slowly
down steep hills to drink
the waters of the wild Upper Umqua.
In a small clearing in the small
carved ravine of a feeder stream
we camp, pitching our tent
in the perfect stillness of the shadows
of the Klamath Indians. Far off,
almost in a dream, the logging trucks
growl west down through the mountains
toward the mills in Roseburg.

I hold the stakes, you hammer:
"Watch the fingers!"—both laughing.
Both recall, in easy conversation,
one-man poncho tents rigged
side by side in total darkness;
always you and I, in iron heat,
in the iron monsoon rains—
not like this at all; and yet,
though years have passed
and we are older by a lifetime,
a simple slip of thought, a pause,
and here: nothing's changed.

For we were never young, it seems,
not then, not ever. I couldn't even cry
the day you went down screaming, angry
jagged steel imbedded in your knee—
I knew you would live,

and I knew you wouldn't be back,
and I was glad, and a little jealous.
Two months later I went down.

We all went down eventually,
the villages aflame, the long
grim lines of soldiers, flotsam
in the vortex of a sinking illusion:
goodbye, Ginny; goodbye, John Kennedy;
goodbye, Tom Paine and high school history—
though here we are still, you and I.
We live our lives now
in a kind of awkward silence
in the perfect stillness of the shadows
of the Klamath Indians.

And I am truly happy
to be with you again. We stand
on the rocks; you point to clear
patches between white water
where the shadows of sleek fish slip,
effortless streaks of energy.
I'm clumsy: with an old, eager patience
you teach me how to cast the fly
gently, so it rides on the surface
with the current, far downstream—
till the rod bends, springs back,
bends again: strike! Your excitement
rises above the river like a wild
song the Douglas firs bend
imperceptibly to hear: shouts,
advice, encouragement, half an hour
and a fourteen-inch rainbow trout
panting hard, eyes alive, its tiny heart
beating with defiance still unbroken

though I hold the fish
helpless in my hands.

I throw the fish back
in the awkward silence, and you
slip your arm around my shoulders
gently for a moment, knowing why.

Later we eat from cans,
the rainbow flashing in the fire
reflecting in our eyes, alive:
familiar gestures—fingers burned
by hot tin lids, a mild curse, quiet
laughter, swish of a knifeblade
plunging idly deep into damp earth.
You ask do I remember the little shy
flower who always wore a white *ao dai*,
and I smile across the flames as the river
tumbles through the darkness toward the sea
that laps the shores of Asia.

The wind moves through the Douglas firs,
and in the perfect stillness of the shadows
of the Klamath Indians, we test
our bonds and find them, after all
these years, still sound—knowing
in the awkward silence we will always share
something worth clinging to
out of the permanent past of stillborn dreams:
the ancient, implacable wisdom
of ignorance shattered forever, a new
reverence we were never taught
by anyone we believed, frail hope
we gave each other, communion
made holy by our shame.

You've found religion since then,
a wife, and two children;
I write poems you admire.
The knee's still stiff, like an old
high school football wound,
and I have trouble hearing. We are
both tired, but reluctant to sleep:
both understand we will never
see each other again; once is enough.
The logging trucks have long since
left the mountains in peace;
in the perfect stillness, we can almost
hear the solemn Douglas firs drinking
the waters of the wild Upper Umqua
we have come so far to worship:
together now, in this small circle of light,
we bow our hearts to the shadows
of the Klamath Indians; now,
and always, in our need.

from
The Samisdat Poems

Turning Thirty

It isn't that I fear
growing older—such things as fear,
reluctance or desire
play no part at all
except as light and shadow sweep a hillside
on a Sunday afternoon,
astonishing the eye but passing on
at sunset with the land
still unchanged: the same rocks,
the same trees, tall grass gently drifting—
merely that I do not understand
how my age has come to me
or what it means.

It's almost like some small
forest creature one might find
outside the door some frosty autumn morning,
tired, lame, uncomprehending,
almost calm.
You want to stroke its fur,
pick it up, mend the leg and send it
scampering away—but something
in its eyes says, "No,
this is how I live, and how I die."
And so, a little sad, you let it be.
Later when you look,
the thing is gone.

And just like that these
thirty years have come and gone,
and I do not understand at all

why I see a man
inside the mirror when a small
boy still lives inside this body
wondering
what causes laughter, why
nations go to war, who paints the startling
colors of the rainbow on a gray vaulted sky,
and when I will be old enough
to know.

The Teacher

for my students at Sandy Spring
Friends School, September 1978

A cold moon hangs
cold fire among the clouds,
and I remember colder nights
in hell when men died
in such pale light as this
of fire swift
and deadly as a heart of ice.

Hardly older then
than you are now,
I hunched down shaking
like an old man
alone in an empty cave
among the rocks of ignorance
and malice honorable men
call truth.

Out of that cave I carried
anger like a torch
to keep my heart from freezing,
and a strange new thing called
love
to keep me sane.

A dozen years ago,
before I ever knew you,
beneath a moon not unlike
this moon tonight,
I swore an oath to teach you

all I know—
and I know things
worth knowing.

It is a desperate future
I cling to,
and it is yours.
All that I have lived for
since that cold moon long ago
hangs in the balance—
and I keep fumbling for words,
but this clip-clapper tongue
won't do.

I am afraid;
I do not want to fail:

I need your hands to steady me;
I need your hearts to give me courage;
I need you to walk with me
until I find a voice
that speaks the language
that you speak.

Companions

Older than ancient, you shadow me
like some puzzled persistent companion.
Wherever I go, whatever I do,
you are there gazing over my shoulder
wide-eyed, bent forward from the hips,
your broad brows furrowed in thought,
long arms gently swaying.

The simplest things amaze you:
when I eat with a fork, your hands
open and close in clumsy imitation;
when I pull on my boots, you
paw at them softly, rocking
back on your haunches, wide lips
stretched in a kind of grin;
you ride in the back seat of my car
terrified, cowering down in a corner.

Yet you swing from the branches of trees
graceful and light as a cat, scampering
over the earth swiftly, agile, alert
to every sound and odor on the wind.
You understand fire, pointing in awe
to the thin flames of hot light,
prodding the coals with a stick,
chattering explanations in your
strange gutteral tongue.

You mourn for the dead;
I have heard your heartbroken howl
piercing the night beneath the new moon.

51

You know what it means to be lonely.

Feeling the undefinable pull
of the dark centuries rising between us
like tides, you huddle inside your cave
with the small fire leaping against the walls
and the glowing eyes of jackals
dotting the black mouth like stars.
The young burrow deeply into your fur.
On the threshold of sleep, you peer
far into the night, awaiting the first
signs of light in the eastern sky—
and I am the bright gleam leaping
deep in your eyes.

Last of the Hard-hearted Ladies

I was always afraid of you—
other grandmothers lovingly
baked pies for grandchildren;
you kicked my ass
for leaving socks on the floor:
it made no sense—

until that day, fifteen,
and no one home but you,
I asked you for a cigarette,
and you said yes,
and talked with me all afternoon
as though I were a man,
and never told a soul.

Years later, I understood
you'd simply always seen the man
leaving socks on the floor
and coats on chairs, and all
you'd ever asked
is that I see it too.

Oh, you bitched about my hair
and my moustache, never liked
my politics: that socialistic crap—
but you grinned like the devil
when I held my ground.

I didn't say a word today
when Dad and Uncle Merv
read that stuff from the Bible

you'd scoffed at all your life,
remembering the times we'd sat
listening to the hymns in church
next door, smoking cigarettes:

they think their faith will help you,
and maybe it will, and anyway
it can't hurt—and the grief,
at least, is real.

So don't be angry with me, Grandma:
if I'd had it our way,
I'd have lit up another cigarette
and passed it to you.

Sunset

Dresden Nuclear Power Station
Morris, Illinois

Late afternoon: in the stillness
before evening, a car on the road
between cornfields surrounding
Dresden Station raises a plume
of dust, and a light wind
settles the dust over the corn.
Power lines over the cornfields
audibly sing the power of cities
beyond sight, where neon lights flash
tomorrow, laughter and dreams.
Deep within Dresden Station,
human beings tamper with atoms.

Dresden: say it, and the air
fills with the wail of sirens,
thin fingers of light
frantically probing the clouds,
red bursting anger, black thunder,
steel drone of the heavy bombers,
dry bones rattle of falling bombs:
    deliver us from fire;
    deliver us from the flames;
    Lord, have mercy upon us.
135,000 human beings
died in the flames of Dresden.

The air to the west is on fire.
The lake to the west burns red
with the sun's descending fire.

The sky rises out of the lake gold
to copper to deep blue, falling
gently away, black, to the east.
Deep within Dresden Station,
human beings tamper with atoms.
Light wind rustles the cornstalks,
the sound like the rustle of skirts
on young graceful women.

from
Matters of the Heart

Again, Rehoboth

I have stood by this bay before.
I have watched the light from the moon
dance in the eyes of friends
while the moon danced on black water,
wanting to know where you were,
exactly what you were thinking.

There was a time when I thought
a man could suffocate
in the dark abscess of want,
a time when I didn't believe
tomorrow would come
except in the shape I gave it.

You belong to that time—you
and the tears that fell in the wake
of the false peace of October
when it still seemed possible
to wield light like a sword.

I am a teacher now;
I live alone.
I am anchored to this world
by all cold necessity
holds sacred: water, salt,
the labored rhythms of breathing.

I cherish my friends,
whose thin threads spread like glowing wires
out from the center, bending away
over the four horizons

in smooth unbroken lines,
and the quiet slap of the water
kissing the land.

When did the recognition come—
the slow submission of dreams; the wind
turning to blow down the years
like a steady silence—
things seem hardly to have changed
at all: these hands; this head
with its wild brown mane;
this heart still beating.

Evening approaches; already
the first star burns in the east.
There will be no moon tonight.
Out on the bay, the boats beat home
to the seagulls' plaintive cries,
their smooth bending sails
blood-red from a fire sun.

Fog

Snow all night, and then the temperature
up fifteen degrees before dawn:
white slush, wet sludge beneath,
not fit for anything—not even children;
and the fog curtaining up from the ground
luminous, so thick you have to part it
as you walk, and duck quickly
under branches out of nowhere.
You know today the sun is shining
somewhere, but it isn't here.

Here, the day is wrapped tightly
in a white shroud shivering thoughts
out of places no one ever visits
on an ordinary day, though admission
price is cheap and never varies:
see yourself the way you really are—
the way, at least, light bent through fog
makes you seem when all reassurances
are gone, it's Sunday, you live alone,
and even the telephone won't ring. Funny

how the good seems nebulous as fog.
Wrong ways, wrong words, wrong decisions
hammer like a blacksmith on an anvil:
people you will never see again come back
real as people you will have to face tomorrow—
and if you've done it wrong, you've done it
wrong so many times it hurts to be alone
on days like this with thirty years of flaws
and nothing in the house but bourbon.

A long, a very long day. Well,
it's good bourbon in any case, and it's
evening now. Snow and mud are freezing,
fog is lifting: clear sky, perhaps,
by morning. So you go to sleep
listening to the silence broken
only by the hammer, waiting
for an ordinary day to set you straight.

The Eruption of Mount St. Helens

for Nimimosha of the Bear Tribe Medicine Society

"Ash fallout is the hot news here."
Too far away to feel or hear the blast,
Nimimosha watched the gray-brown cloud
rising and advancing east
until the land and all living things
lay blanketed in ash, and her daughter's
infant eyes burned red with grit,
then she went inside.

"If it rains lightly now," she writes,
"the ash will turn to caustic paste
and harden to dissolve slowly,
burning the earth as it goes.
We're concerned about the fish"—
jellied mud on surfaces of ponds
and lakes, blocking oxygen exchange;
"the cows are eating ash-coated grass,
drinking ash-coated water,
blinking ash-coated eyes.
Then there are the horses. . . .

"We must stay inside.
The highways all around Spokane
are blocked; telephones are down;
everything is closed. We're thankful

"things are not too bad; even though
the day turned black at noon, the world
continues, and we're all still here.

63

The feeling here is powerful.
Walk in balance on Mother Earth."

My ash-coated heart soars
to where she is—as if desire alone
could lift the burden of her hardship,
clean the water, feed the cows, wipe
the burning grit from Yarroe's eyes—
and yet I cannot cry:

Nature's fury lacks the malice
of seashore wildlife sanctuaries
smothering in oil from sinking tankers,
or an Indochinese village disappearing
in an orange ball of napalm, or a lake
dying from the mills in Buffalo,
or the slums of Baltimore.

I will not cry for Nimimosha:
St. Helens is the throat of Mother Earth,
and the violence is Her song—
and there is no sadness in it.

The Grim Art of Teaching

Don't look at me
with those woman's eyes
and that burgeoning womanhood bursting
out of clothes just made
for walking into classrooms:
Stop the show! Who cares
about Shakespeare, anyway?

Don't smile, don't stare, don't
tell me I'm cute, and don't make jokes
about meeting after school
that don't sound funny.

I'm damned near old enough
to be your father;
you're damned near old enough
to be my lover;
this is one damned dangerous way
to make a living—
and the Devil is the headmaster.

Matters of the Heart

for Thomas McGrath & James Cooney

Old Tom, your rasping low voice
is so soft it's hard to imagine machinegun
bullets among the strikers in New Orleans
or the hard clubs on soft round heads
by the docks in New York City;
Jim, shuffling along with your walking stick
like an angry shepherd, kind as a good Samaritan,
first American printer of Miller and Nin:

"The deepest part of a man is his sense
of essential truth, essential honour, essential
justice: they hated him because he was free,
because he wasn't cowed as they were . . ."

"Wild talk, and easy enough now to laugh.
That's not the point and never was the point:
What was real was the generosity, expectant hope,
The open and true desire to create the good."

You rascals. What am I supposed to do?
Storm the White House? Picket Chase Manhattan?
What? I've tried it all, believe me; nothing
works. Everyone's asleep, or much too busy.

The point is: things are different now.
In the age of the MX missile and the Trident
nuclear submarine and the 20-megaton bomb
multiplied by a couple of thousand or so,
what are the odds I'll ever see
the same age you are now?

Did it seem so bleak in 1940
in that awful twilight when half the world
plunged headlong into darkness
out of the decade of comradeship and hope
while the other half stood poised to follow?

Four more decades have passed since then,
and you're still at it. The Pole Star's gone;
even the dreams we steered by only ten years ago
are gone. Where do you get your strength?

I'm tired of being swatted like a bothersome fly:
pariah, voice in the wilderness. My friends
look at me with pity in their eyes.
I want to own a house, raise a family,
draw a steady paycheck. What, after all, can I do
to change the course of a whole mad world?
I'm only a man; I want to forget for awhile
and be happy . . .
                    . . . and yet your lives,
your words, your breath, your beating
old tired fighters' unbowed hearts
boom through the stillness of excuses
like a stuck clock forever tolling:

"Don't give in. Go on. Keep on.
Resist. Keep on. Go on."

Briana

for CJ, in memory of Jill

Death comes knocking and the silence descends
like a black bird alighting on the windowledge
on a black night with no candles.

Yet everything continues: bottle time,
nap time, play time, bath time, story time,
bed time—only a brief confusion:
for a few days you asked for mommy;
then you stopped asking.

You can't know the black bird will sit
for a lifetime in your father's heart.
I watch him with you now:
the tall slender frame
bending over your crib like a willow;
the large hands hesitantly poised—
wanting to touch,
not wanting to wake you;
the soft searching eyes permanently puzzling
an incomprehensible absence
he will never let you feel
if he can help it.

Years will pass before you understand
the secret tremble when your father holds you,
just how much such a small child weighs—
but that's okay;
                    don't trouble your dreams

with wondering. Be what you are:
your mother's daughter. Be a candle.

Light the awful silence with your laughter.

from
*To Those Who Have Gone
Home Tired*

Channel Fever

When I cast off in my small boat
with its one sail white and yellow
brilliant in the sunlight, I thought
I heard the sea calling in a soft song
sweet as any mermaid sings to sailors
in their dreams. I disappeared after it
into that vastness searching, searching.

I have caught fish to feed myself,
throwing the offal and bones to the sharks,
eating the meat raw, washing it down
with rainwater collected in a tin cup.

I never imagined it would be so lonely.
At times I have been delirious:
tearing the tattered remnants of my clothes,
shouting at stars, fighting to keep
from pitching myself headlong into the sea.

The dolphins, at least, were real; sometimes
on bright days they paced my small boat,
breasting the waves, laughing—or at night,
their sleek gray bodies luminescent green
in phosphorescent moonlight. For awhile,
I thought it was their song I followed—
but the wind blew too steady for that;
the wind drove my small boat always
over the next wave, and over the next wave.

When I first smelled land, I didn't believe it.
"Is this what it means to be mad?" I thought.

But my small boat surged suddenly forward,
and the seabirds riding the waves suddenly
surged up screaming and whirling in great
wheeling circles of excitement—and I know now,
as any sailor does even before the long voyage

is over, all along it was your
invisible hand on the tiller, your
breath beating my small boat steadily on
toward the harbor shaped like a heart.
It was you.
It is your song I heard.

The Invasion of Grenada

I didn't want a monument,
not even one as sober as that
vast black wall of broken lives.
I didn't want a postage stamp.
I didn't want a road beside the Delaware
River with a sign proclaiming:
"Vietnam Veterans Memorial Highway."

What I wanted was a simple recognition
of the limits of our power as a nation
to inflict our will on others.
What I wanted was an understanding
that the world is neither black-and-white
nor ours.

What I wanted
was an end to monuments.

from
The Outer Banks

The Farmer

Each day I go into the fields
to see what is growing
and what remains to be done.
It is always the same thing: nothing
is growing; everything needs to be done.
Plow, harrow, disc, water, pray
till my bones ache and hands rub
blood-raw with honest labor—
all that grows is the slow
intransigent intensity of need.
I have sown my seed on soil
guaranteed by poverty to fail.

But I don't complain—except
to passersby who ask me why
I work such barren earth.
They would not understand me
if I stooped to lift a rock
and hold it like a child, or laughed,
or told them it is their poverty
I labor to relieve. For them,
I complain. A farmer of dreams
knows how to pretend. A farmer of dreams
knows what it means to be patient.
Each day I go into the fields.

Gifts

for Anne Gulick Ehrhart

I give you the worst gift first
as a warning: the sullen silence
awakening in the morning; the self-
centered dolt too blunt sometimes
to button his own trousers;
the quick tongue slashing;
the perpetual anger at being
perpetually mortal.

The second gift I give you
of necessity: the come-what-may;
the kiss on the cheek on the way
out the door, real and mindless
as superstition; rumpled clothes,
broken dishes, grocery bills;
the guarantee of disagreements;
the mundane goings and comings
of daily routine.

But the third gift is a promise,
and I give it also to you: a warm
heart constantly beating;
a companion; warm arms, warm lips,
laughter brighter than mountain fire,
tears as wild as the sea;
the unrelenting desire to please;
an unrelenting struggle to know;
unrepentant exuberant love
for as long as we share this earth.

27 June 1981

Continuity

Because I love my wife, I've traveled
six hundred miles to stand for fifteen minutes
by a cold stone standing in a grove of pines
in West Tisbury, Martha's Vineyard, Massachusetts.
What are you to me? A name. A few
silent photographs I've seen in albums.
Second-hand stories. I never even met you.

The taxi idles by the graveyard gate;
a cold Atlantic wind whips the pines.
Your daughter grips my arm—once, twice, hard:
"My mother died!" she cries, as though the news
had just arrived, the tears standing for a moment
in her eyes before they topple down her face.
I think of mothers, think of death, and love

and all at once my throat constricts
in startled grief; my own tears rise:
mother of my wife, your living soul
breathes in every gesture of your daughter,
and your daughter is the touchstone of my life.
Because I love my wife, I've traveled
six hundred miles to discover that I miss you,
and to thank you for the splendid child you raised.

New Jersey Pine Barrens

Sixty miles away, in New York City,
herds of cars stampede down avenues,
animated lumps of steel and fumes.
Thirty miles away, in Philadelphia,
a mugger steals a purse in broad daylight
from a screaming old woman on Broad Street.
Here, I wake to whippoorwills and bullfrogs.

Swamp cedar, scrub oak, stunted maple
whisper as I ready the canoes
beside the beaver dam on Batsto River.
The children on the school camping trip
are still asleep. A beaver tail slaps.
I urinate beside a blueberry bush,
notice white violent and lady slipper,
pickerel gliding through the quiet pond.

Soon the children will awake, all energy.
Alien and graceless in their sleek canoes,
they will spend this day ricocheting
off sunken stumps and overhanging trees,
heaping angry blame for faulty navigation
on anyone but self, their adolescent
piping shrieks splitting the awesome
silence with a day-long jagged gash.

Too young to understand, their thoughts
are all of who-rammed-who, and the hot-faced
shame of looking clumsy. I cup my hand,
dip it in the beaver pond and drink

the majesty of wilderness, wondering
how much longer will it be
before children like these will have to learn
the majesty of wilderness
from books.

Pagan

for the people of El Salvador

In the heart of the night
that beats in the heart of the people,
something is waking
out of the half-sleep
of centuries.
Beckoned alive
by the endless nightmare of priests,
viceroys and chains,
the pestilence of toil
and submission,
where nothing has ever been sacred
but gold,
greed,
and the lash,
it rears its slow black head
and blinks its eyes open.
Its wings unfold
like the slow seepage of blood
from a festering wound:
thunder and clouds
are among the stars.
Slowly it rises
on the rising wind,
the hard white tips
of its fangs
catching the moon.

A Warning to My Students

George School
November 1981

The B-1 bomber
is going to be built
after all: not scrapped, after all
our resistance; just postponed.
"Necessity requires. . . ,"
yet another president insists;
the secretary of state discusses
limited nuclear war
as if it were sane;
and in El Salvador, another
petty upper-class junta
needs American aid
to fight the communists.

What happened
to the last twenty years?

If I were young again,
I could do it all
differently: go to college,
go to Canada, live underground
on the lam in basement apartments
in strange cities—anything
but kill
somebody else's enemies
for somebody else's reasons.

And now I see it all
coming

one more time; one
by one, all the old flags
resurrected
and ready
for the rockets' red glare
still another time—
and I wake up nights, afraid,
and I have to reach out
and touch my wife,
just to make sure.

Sometimes she wakes up, too.
"It's all right," she says;
she strokes my head;
"It's just a dream."

And she's right, too:
these days, for me
it's just a dream

because the next time they come looking
for soldiers, they won't come looking
for me. I'm too old;
I know too much.

The next time they come looking
for soldiers, they'll come looking
for you.

Sound Advice

Remember the time Jerry Doughty
beat you up for no good reason
on the ice at Sellersville while all
the other kids stood around and laughed?
You skated home alone that day, swearing
you would find a way to even up the score.
But you never did: years passed,
he moved away, your adolescent pride
still tucked beneath his belt like a trophy.

Or one year later, in the fifth grade,
when Margie Strawser told the teacher
you had hit her with a bean-shooter?
Nothing you protested mattered:
the shooter and the beans were in your desk.
You got paddled as the whole class watched,
and Margie got an A in citizenship.

You should have learned something
growing up. Instead, you volunteered.
And when you found your war as rotten
as the rotting corpses of the dead
peasants lying in the green rice
they would never harvest, you were shocked
that nothing you protested mattered.
Thirteen years have passed since then,
and still your anger rises at the way people
turn away from what you have to say.

Who taught you to believe in words?
Listen: injustice is a fact.
Like dust rising when the wind blows.

Like heat when the fire rises.
A natural thing. The white space
between the lines of every history
book you've ever read. The back side
of the Golden Rule. The one unbroken law.

And yet you've quit a half a dozen jobs
on principle: point of order! Point of order—
as though you think it matters more than bread.
Everywhere you go, the blade of your contempt
draws blood. No wonder people hate you.
Listen, friend: don't make us so uncomfortable.
We don't like it any more than you do,
but the world is what it is. You can't change it.
Face it. Learn to bend. We have.

Everett Dirksen, His Wife, You & Me

I read once that Everett Dirksen,
United States Senator, never slept
a night without his wife of fifty years.
One can almost see them, near the end:
two doddering old white-haired giggling
lovers climbing into bed, the undimmed
passion still glowing steadily from within—
enough to light the darkness one more night.

And yet I think that light was raised
against a darker darkness both, perhaps,
saw approaching years before the end.
I see it coming, too—saw it years
before I met you; it scared me then,
and still does, and you're the only one
who's ever made me feel the weight
a little less. We giggle, too, sometimes.

One might marvel at the long-enduring
passion of that husband and his wife:
fifty years without a night alone;
marvelous, indeed—
but it's other couples who amaze me:
their ignorance, their faith, their sheer
bravado. Whether we shall be together
or alone in death, I have no way of knowing;

but I know the weight, and how it feels
to pass the night without you.

Cowgirls, Teachers & Dreams

for Betsy in Montana

That day we fished Coyote Creek
from Pete's ranch to the upper barn,
dry pale prairie grass rippled
pastures mile on mile to mountains
shouldering sky. Cattle grazed the high
plateaus where men in winter still
go mad from loneliness and snow. Hard
land, its beauty self-composed; a long
way from anywhere. We shared one rod.
You showed me where the best spots were,
parted bushes—"Shhh," you said, "don't
scare the fish"—coached my clumsy casts.
It didn't help: you caught twenty; I
caught none. It didn't matter. Seven
hours working up the creek through
morning into afternoon toward evening.
Words passed softly back and forth
like dry prairie grass in wind. Magic
how that hot dry day in summer in Montana
passed so gently. At the upper barn,
we cleaned the fish: you deftly lopped
off heads and tails, taught me how
to slit their bellies, poke my finger
down the spines to clear the guts in one
swift stroke. How was I to tell you
I was squeamish? Biting flesh inside
my mouth, I did as I was shown. "It's late,"
you said, "we'd better take the horse."
How was I to tell you I was scared

of horses, hadn't ridden since that day
when I was ten and rode four wild miles
on a horse that wasn't stable-broken?
I climbed up behind you: no saddle,
nothing but your slender waist to hold—
a stalk of prairie grass in wind—and you
went straight for every ditch you saw,
jumping, laughing: "Hang on tight!"—stopping
only when you saw the mother antelope
and fauns, babies still with spots, all
three staring, undecided. Maybe next time
bobcats or wolves instead of riders.
The cook got fired while we fished.
Drinking on the job. A hard life in Big
Sky Country. I was only passing through;
I've never seen you since. Not that I
would have a reason: you were eight, and I
was twenty-two. The friends I stopped
to see were only summer help—married now,
a lawyer and a teacher in the East.
I'm a teacher, too. So were you.
And in my mind, you'll always catch
the fattest trout and ride the swiftest
horse, always stop to gaze at fauns,
and never lose your innocence or courage
in that lonely hard land you offered
to a stranger like a treasure,
like a blessing.

". . . the light that cannot fade . . ."

Suzie, you picked a hell of a time
to teach me about mortality.
I was in North Carolina then,
talking tough, eating from cans,
wearing my helmet John Wayne style—
and you were suddenly dead:
a crushed skull on a pre-dawn road
just two weeks shy of college,
and me about to leave for Vietnam.

I wanted you and me alive;
I wanted out.
That night I cried till dawn.

Funny, how I managed to survive
that war, how the years have passed,
how I'm thirty-four and getting on,
and how your death
bestowed upon my life a permanence
I never would have had
if you had lived:

you'd have gone to college,
married some good man from Illinois,
and disappeared like all the other
friends I had back then who meant
so much and whom I haven't
thought about in years.

But as it is, I think of you
whenever dancers flow across a stage

or graceful gymnasts balance on the beam.
And every time I think of you,
you're young.

(for Carolyn Sue Brenner, 1948-1966)

Responsibility

The Congress shall have power to lay
and collect taxes . . . to . . . provide for
the common defense and general welfare
of the United States.
—Article I, Section 8, Paragraph 1
United States Constitution

The sun taps on the kitchen table;
coffee boils. As birds awaken
trees beyond the window, I think of you
upstairs: your naked body curled
around a pillow, your gentle face
an easy dream of last night's love.
It's Friday; summer.

Somewhere
in another country to the south,
government troops are stalking
through a nightmare; a naked body
in the dusty street behind them
sprawls in rubbish, and a woman
in a house with the door kicked in
pounds fists on empty walls. There,
the news is always bad, the soldiers
always armed, the people
always waiting for the sound
of boots splintering wood.

What if you and I were wrenched from sleep
by soldiers, and they dragged me out
and shot me? Just like that; just
the way it happens every day:
the life we share,

all the years ahead we savor
like the rich taste of good imported coffee,
vanished
in a single bloody hole between the eyes.

Would you fix the door and go on living?
Or would the soldiers rape and shoot you, too?
Idle thoughts. Things like that don't happen
in America. The sun climbs;
the coffee's gone; time to leave for work.
Friday, payday, security:
money in my pocket for the weekend;
money for my government;
money for the soldiers of El Salvador,
fifty bullets to the box.

The Blizzard of Sixty-six

Snow came early here, and hard:
roads treacherous; wires down.
School authorities should have cancelled
the annual high school Christmas dance:
two couples died on the way home.
"Tragedy!" the local papers declared,
but the snow kept falling.

Somewhere in a folder in a file
is a photograph of me in a uniform:
one stripe for PFC; girl in a yellow gown.
I took her home through the falling snow,
kissed goodnight, and left for Asia.

All through that long year, snow
fell and fell on the green rice,
on gray buffalo, thatched huts, green
patrols, and the mounting yellow dead.

Randy, class of '65, died
in terminal cold in the Mekong Delta;
Kenny, class of '66, died in a blizzard
of lead in the Central Highlands;
I came home with permanent chills,
the yellow nameless dead of Asia
crammed into my seabag, and all of us
looking for a reason.

We never found one. Presidents
come and go away like snowdrifts

in driveways; generals come and go;
the earth goes on silently turning
and turning through its seasons,
and the snow keeps falling.

The Vision

It can happen anywhere:
on a bus, on the street,
on a soft afternoon standing
by an old spring the first Maryland
Quakers quenched their thirst at
after a hard day in the fields;
at work—often at work—in the midst
of the dull ache of moving
from day to day; over a beer;
in the arms of the person you love.

Maybe a flower will trigger it off—
its fiery petals, yellow and orange,
dancing the breeze like cobweb;
or a girl's shy smile and hesitant
sparkling eyes; an aroma
that conjures a memory;
or the snatch of a song,
or a touch, or a word, or silence—

and the heart leaps up
like the first glimpse of the cloudless
moonless night sky above New Mexico,
and you suddenly stare
into the infinite power
of how things could be
if the dreams you live on
came true.

Only a flash,
a single terrible instant,

lifting and swift as lightning,
an explosion of joy—

and then it is gone,
and only the vision remains.

And the longing.

from The Outer Banks

1.

Hysterical seagulls dart and soar
through evening's rising calm. Some alight
and strut like tiny generals among the children
chasing spindly ghost crabs on the beach.
Here, a fisherman. There, two lovers sharing secrets.
And there a kite, riding a stiff sea breeze
that makes the dune grass ripple and toss
like slow green rollers just before they burst,
exploding phosphorescent white on dark wet sand.
A half-mile south, Cape Hatteras light, its tower
spiraled black and white, begins to flash
in deepening twilight. Stars appear.
The flash atop Cape Hatteras light becomes a soft
revolving beam casting silver light on rooftops,
dune tops, sand and surf, then skittering over waves
and out to sea.
Returning.
Gone again.
And back.
And gone.
A perpetual circle of moving light.
An all-night silent song.

7.

Near rushes in a marshy pond in Buxton Woods,
an egret, like solemn elder of the realm,
stands alone knee-deep in water. The posture
of the bird suggests a kind of wisdom,
or a perfect inner calm. Behind the bird,
beyond the woods, the black and white spiral
of the lighthouse rises. Bird and lighthouse;
blue sky; the silence of the whispered afternoon.
An old road, a rutted double sand-track
long overgrown, passes by the pond and disappears
through loblolly pines toward old abandoned houses.
A bare breath of wind disturbs the rushes:
the black beak turns; the stilt-like legs
take two steps forward; the slow broad wings
unfold. The great bird flies.

8.

Stand on the beach at night at Cape Hatteras
looking east across the water. Keep watching:
there!   Flash.   Flash.
That's the beacon on the Texas Tower
marking the outer edge of Diamond Shoals.

The buoys placed on Diamond Shoals
washed away in a storm.
The lightship stationed on the shoals
broke loose and wrecked in a storm.
The floating bell beacon disappeared.
More buoys washed away.

The Diamond Shoals lighthouse project
ended in a storm before completion.
Another lightship stationed on the shoals
broke loose and wrecked in a storm.
A German U-boat sank another.

Look again at the flashing light.
Look at the darkness between the flashes.
Look at the waiting sea.

10.

The sea breeze gently rubs the dunes. The sky
is clear. The beach is empty now of children,
fishers, fires, and kites. Only the lovers,
huddled down for shelter in the hollow of a dune,
stay to watch the light revolving, listening
to its song. What secrets do they share
as night moves on toward dawn? Ageless secrets.
Timeless secrets. Listen to their muffled giggles
drifting on the air. This is how it always is
because all lovers think themselves
immortal. How else could we go on?
Cape Hatteras light casts silver light on rooftops,
dunetops, sand and surf, skittering over waves
and out to sea.
Returning.
Gone again.
And back.
And gone.

from
Winter Bells

Winter Bells

In the dark breath of February,
how your voice lightly rises
over clouds, cold rain, the first
flat gray of early dawn,
lifting me into another day.
Small miracle, such magic.

I almost died in February,
Hue City, 1968; and once I drove
non-stop for twenty-two hours
all the way to Coconut Grove
just to escape the cold,
such fear I have of cold

and the aching emptiness like cold;
February, so empty of dreams,
so like the life I labored through
season by slow season.
Who would have thought a single
voice could change the natural world

or my unnatural fear
of short days and a long life?
Woman with voice like a carillon
pealing the cold from my bones.

POW/MIA

I. In the jungle of years,
   lost voices are calling. Long
   are the memories,
   bitterly long the waiting,
   and the names of the missing and dead
   wander
   disembodied
   through a green tangle
   of rumors and lies,
   gliding like shadows among vines.

II. Somewhere, so the rumors go,
    men still live in jungle prisons.
    Somewhere in Hanoi, the true believers
    know,
    the bodies of four hundred servicemen
    lie on slabs of cold
    communist hate.

III. Mothers, fathers,
     wives and lovers,
     sons and daughters,
     touch your empty fingers to your lips
     and rejoice
     in your sacrifice and pain:
     your loved ones' cause
     was noble,
     says the state.

IV. In March of 1985, the wreckage
    of a plane was found in Laos.

Little remained of the dead:
rings, bone chips, burned
bits of leather and cloth;
for thirteen families,
twenty years of hope
and rumors
turned acid on the soul
by a single chance discovery.

V. Our enemies are legion,
   says the state;
   let bugles blare
   and bang the drum slowly,
   bang the drum.

VI. God forgive me, but I've seen
    that triple-canopied green
    nightmare of a jungle
    where a man in a plane could go down
    unseen, and never be found
    by anyone.
    Not ever.
    There are facts,
    and there are facts:
    when the first missing man
    walks alive out of that green tangle
    of rumors and lies,
    I shall lie
    down silent as a jungle shadow,
    and dream the sound of insects
    gnawing bones.

Parade

New York City
May 7th, 1985

Ten years after the last rooftop
chopper out of Saigon.

Ten, fifteen, twenty years
too late for kids not twenty
years old and dead in ricefields;
brain-dead, soul-dead, half-dead
in wheelchairs. Even the unmarked
forever Absent Without Leave.

You'd think that any self-respecting
vet would give the middle finger
to the folks who thought of it
ten years and more too late—

yet there they were: the sad
survivors, balding, overweight
and full of beer, weeping, grateful
for their hour come round at last.

I saw one man in camouflaged utilities;
a boy, his son, dressed like dad;
both proudly marching.

How many wounded generations,
touched with fire, have offered up
their children to the gods of fire?
Even now, new flames are burning,

and the gods of fire call for more,
and the new recruits keep coming.

What fire will burn that small
boy marching with his father?
What parade will heal
his father's wounds?

For Mrs. Na

Cu Chi District
December 1985

I always told myself,
if I ever got the chance to go back,
I'd never say "I'm sorry"
to anyone. Christ,

those guys I saw on television once:
sitting in Hanoi, the cameras rolling,
crying, blubbering
all over the place. Sure,

I'm sorry. I never meant
to do the things I did.
But that was nearly twenty years ago:
enough's enough.

If I ever go back,
I always told myself,
I'll hold my head steady
and look them in the eye.

But here I am at last—
and here you are.
And you lost five sons in the war.
And you haven't any left.

And I'm staring at my hands
and eating tears,
trying to think of something else to say
besides "I'm sorry."

Twice Betrayed

for Nguyen Thi My Huong
Ho Chi Minh City
December 1985

Some American soldier
came to your mother for love,
or lust, a moment's respite from loneliness,
and you happened. Fourteen years later,
I meet you on the street at night
in the city that was once called Saigon,
and you are almost a woman,
barefooted, dressed in dirty clothes,
beautiful with your one shy dimple.

It doesn't really matter who won;
either way, you were always destined
to be one of the losers:
if he wasn't killed, your father left
for the place we used to call The World
years before the revolution's tanks
crushed the gates of the old regime forever.

Now we sit on a bench in a crowded park
burdened by history. It isn't easy
being here again after all these years.
I marvel at your serenity—but of course,
you can't possibly know who I am,
or how far I have come to be here.
You only know that I look like you,
that together we are outcasts.

And so we converse in gestures and signs

and the few words we can both understand,
and for now it almost seems enough
just to discover ways to make you smile.

But it isn't, and I have no way
to tell you that I cannot stay here
and I cannot take you with me.
I will tell my wife about you.
I will put your photograph on my desk.
I will dream you are my own daughter.
But none of that will matter
when you come here tomorrow
and I'm gone.

Adoquinas

for the old man

I never thought I'd see the day
Samoza would be gone. But God
helps those who help themselves.
Somoza helped us, too.
Oh, yes. That's the best part.
After the earthquake, Somoza decreed
all the streets and roads
be paved with *adoquinas*. Somoza
owned the *adoquina* factory.
He made a fortune
selling *adoquinas* to himself.
So after we had finally
had enough, we tore the streets
and roads apart and used
Somoza's *adoquinas* for our barricades.
These we used to stop Somoza's
armored cars. We did this here,
in Masaya, in this very street.
Then our fighters killed Somoza's
Guardsmen with their homemade bombs.
We had nothing, but we won.
And I'll tell you why:
look at the belltower.
You think those holes are bulletholes,
but they're the wounds of Christ.
I've even seen them bleed.

Why I Don't Mind Rocking
Leela to Sleep

Sitting at night on the porch
with my daughter asleep in my arms,
I thought I heard a rifle shot—
that singular crack
with no past
and a future chiseled in stone.

It was only a car,
but the memory of bullets
shivered a cold hole tunneling
half the distance to dawn.

*

Once, when I was a boy,
standing alone in my father's church
amid the rows of polished pews,
ponderous oak beams pushing
the darkened ceiling aloft, a Jesus
larger than life knocking softly
at the door to the heart
of the stained-glass window
lit by a distant streetlamp,
I heard a voice,
and I thought it was God.
It terrified me home to fitful sleep.

Strange God, to sing such a voice
in the heart of a small child.
But the world is a strange creation,
and now my own small child
cries out in her sleep,
and I wonder what she is dreaming
and what she has heard.

*

What hurts most
is the plodding sameness
of cruelty, a circular world
impervious to change,
the grinding erosion of hope
stripping the soul.
These days, it almost seems enough
just to accomplish the household chores
and still be ready for work.

*

What I want for my daughter
she shall never have:
a world without war, a life
untouched by bigotry or hate,
a mind free to carry a thought
up to the light of pure possibility.

She should be young forever.
I could hold her here in my arms
and offer her comfort,

115

a place to rest,
the illusion, at least, of shelter.
I don't want her
ever to be alone in a world
with the Gentle Shepherd
frozen in glass and the voice
of a pitiless, idiot god
chasing her down the years.

What Keeps Me Going

Pressed down by the weight
of despair, I could sit for hours
idly searching the ashes
from my cigarette, the darkness
of silos, the convoluted paths
we have followed into this morass
of disasters just waiting to happen,

but my daughter needs to sleep
and wants me near. She knows
nothing of my thoughts. Not one
missile mars her questioning
inspection of my eyes; she wants
only the assurance of my smile,
the familiar placed just so:

Brown Bear, Thumper Bunny, Clown.
These are the circumference
of her world. She sucks her thumb,
rubs her face hard against the mattress,
and begins again
the long night dreaming
darkness into dawn.

from
Just for Laughs

Just for Laughs

When I was ten, I thought that I
would live forever, I could kill
whatever I pleased, I was all
that mattered. How else
can one explain the firecrackers
stuffed down throats of frogs and lit:
hop, hop, boom! A lot of laughs.

Once we found a plump snake
sunning itself beside the creek.
Sluggish in the early morning
chill, it only raised its head
and turned two diamond-black eyes
to see four small boys with sticks.

It didn't understand until we
started beating on its flanks
that we were dangerous
and it was trapped.
Our sticks were too light
and we too timid to inflict
anything but fury, so we
started throwing stones.

Small gashes ripped that snake's
fat thrashing sides until it
finally tired, though it couldn't
run and wouldn't die. It only
lay there heaving as the stones
fell faster—till a miracle

of birth—a miracle of birth
began so strangely even we
were brought up short and stood
there for a moment dumbly watching:

out of those gashes crawled a dozen
baby watersnakes, a dozen more,
small wriggling slivers of their
mother's flesh; some were bleeding,
some had broken backs and dragged
limp tails sideways through the dust.

Premature, even the ones uninjured
that we carried home and put in jars
all died. But it didn't matter.
We had frogs and painted turtles,
salamanders, and a praying mantis.
Years later, I volunteered for war,
still oblivious to what I'd done,
or what I was about to do, or why.

In the Valley of the Shadow

Something made us bolt upright,
all zombie eyes, all ears and nerves.
Something out there in the dark
came breathing, stalking, waiting.

Our fathers, who bequeathed to us
this rotten patch of earth, this fate.
Satan. God. The government.
No matter: it was there and deadly.

All night we hunched in what we wore
like turtles, like the frightened kids
we were and were not anymore,
silent, lost, half-crazed, and deadly,

wanting women, girlfriends, mothers
to protect us, to descend in fire
on angels' wings, torch the darkness,
pluck us from this sad mistake.

No one came. Something stayed there
just beyond our range of vision,
just a shadow on our hearts,
and no one willing to admit

we'd rape our mothers, shoot our fathers,
overthrow the government and swear
our innocence to God or Satan
for a single drop of sun.

Something left us slack-jawed, staring

at our own reflections in the dark:
what we were, what we are, and will be.
Bent, we drag it with us like a cross.

Second Thoughts

for Nguyen Van Hung

You watch with admiration as I roll
a cigarette from papers and tobacco.
Hanoi. The Rising Dragon. 1985.
You can't do what I can do
because it takes two hands

and you have only one, the other
lost years ago somewhere near Laos.
I roll another one for you. You smile,
then shrug, as if deformity from war
were just a minor inconvenience.

Together we discover what we share:
Hue City. Tet. 1968.
Sipping *Lua Moi*, we walk again
familiar ground when you were whole
and I was whole and everything around us

lay in ruins, dead or burning.
But not us. Not you and I. We're partners
in that ugly dance of men
who do the killing and the dying
and survive.

Now you run a factory; I teach and write.
You lost your arm, but have no
second thoughts about the war you fought.
I lost a piece of my humanity,
it's absence heavy as a severed arm—

but there I go again: those second thoughts
I carry always like an empty sleeve
when you are happy just to share
a cigarette and *Lua Moi*, the simple joy
of being with an old friend.

The Origins of Passion

I am eight years old and naked
in my mother's bedroom: lipsticks,
brushes, combs and stockings fragrant
with her blessing hands, the vanity
an altar, I her secret acolyte.
A white lace slip drapes carelessly
across a chair; I take it in my hands,
press my face too deeply in its folds,
lift my trembling arms and drop it
over me, aching with desire
I can't articulate or understand,
immersed in her, burning with loss.

In all the years to come, I will
make love to women smelling softly
of lavender and talc, blessing me
with hands adept at rituals I want
to share but don't know how or why:
lipsticks, brushes, combs and stockings.
I will beg my wife to leave
her slip on; I will press my face
between her breasts and thighs and buttocks
too deeply, burning
to immerse myself in what I love,
still inarticulate, uncomprehending.

A Scientific Treatise for My Wife

The ancients thought the world is flat
and rides upon a turtle's back,
or that the planets, sun and stars
revolve around the earth in crystal spheres.

Thus they defined the universe
till Galileo burst simplicity
by gazing at the heavens with a glass,
confirming Kepler and Copernicus.

All hell broke loose,
churchmen apoplectic, and the renaissance,
and finally Newton to explain it all,
a scientific substitute for Adam's fall.

Not exactly simple, but it worked
till Einstein stumbled on some quirks
in Newton's logic, and explicable
at last evolved incomprehensible.

Not good enough, said Stephen Hawking,
who proceeded to apply his daunting
intellect to postulating ways
black holes disfigure time and space.

He's got a Cambridge Ph.D.;
he's looking for a unifying theory,
and he's covered acres with equations.
Amazing. Centuries of speculation.

Okay, I'm not a physicist.

But even geniuses can miss the obvious,
and I don't need a Ph.D. to know
the universe begins and ends with you.

For Anne, Approaching Thirty-five

Alone in the basement, sorting clothes,
I found that pair of panties I like
(the beige ones with the lacy waist).

I meant to put them in the washer—
but they felt so smooth, so soft, I
just stood there getting hard. Woman,

never mind the crows' feet and creeping slack.
For me, you'll always be sultry,
mysterious, ready for anything.

Some Other World

Was there ever a moment
more perfect than this?
The house all dark, the wind
at the windows, the warmth
of your body against my chest,
and you asleep in my arms.

I thought for awhile
you would never stop crying:
the knife-edged howl, the sucking
gasps, the quivering lower lip—
but I'm learning what troubles
an infant's dreams can be soothed
with patience and time.

Once, before you were born,
I watched for a moment
an egret ascend from a pond
with the grace of a whisper.
And once I dreamed a man
with a rifle refused to take aim;
I awoke to a sadness
deeper than dreams.

And I'm wishing this moment
could last forever; I'm wishing
the things that trouble my dreams
could be kept outside like the wind.

A Small Romance

Suddenly, to your surprise,
I plucked two sapphires from your eyes
and held them to the fading light
like two blue burning stars. Night

was hard upon us, and the snow
fell in sheets beyond the window,
but we were warm in your small bed
and on your pillow, around your head,

a soft blue light seemed to dance.
I held you tight, a small romance
of sleepy child and sleepy father
singing sapphire songs together

in gentle darkness burning blue
until your breath came deep and you
were sleeping, and to my surprise,
I plucked two sapphires from my eyes.

Small Song for Daddy

It isn't like my daughter
to awake at one a.m.—
but here she is.

She pulls the hairs on my chest
idly, wiggles her toes, sighs
almost as if in meditation,
and begins to sing softly,

the language hers alone,
the voice clear and fragile
as water striking stone.

New in a world where new
is all she knows, she sings
for each new wonder
she discovers—as if those

curtains, the chair, that
box of Kleenex were created
solely to delight her.

And they do. And she sings,
not knowing she is singing
for a father much in need
of her particular song.

The Facts of Life

Winter, and a gray storm sea
behaved as if we didn't matter,
driving the main deck under water,
breaking over the flying bridge,
leaving the catwalks slick with ice.
Even our tanker seemed to ignore
its own despair, wallowing
steadily north like a floating brick.

For a night and day we didn't eat
or sleep or change our filthy clothes,
staring into a sky the color of ash,
trying to will the weather to break,
even the old salts studying clouds,
reluctant to meet each other's gaze.
And the freezing rain blown horizontal,
sweeping the decks like shotgun blasts.

Bells down in the engineroom.
The slow finger of moving light
from the lightship off Columbia Bar
barely able to bore a hole
in the smothering darkness. Christ,
why did we ever come to sea?
Where are the whales and porpoises,
the thousand mermaids singing?

Then the ship turned east, Astoria,
the shelter of the river, still
invisible across that deadly patch
of turbulence, the criss-cross waves,
the shifting sandbars just beneath

the surface, tossing steel like cork,
and all of us in life preservers,
hatches battened, portholes battened.

Maybe we would make it over.
Maybe by tomorrow we'd be drinking
beer in bars in downtown Portland.
Maybe we would sail again. Or maybe
we would finally prove what any sailor
understands, the scientists be damned:
the earth is flat, you reach the edge,
fall off, and don't come back.

Love in an Evil Time

for Diana Bedell

There was a woman I knew.
There was a candle, an altar,
a window, soft curves and shadows.
Miracles stirred in her eyes:

that she could raise the dead;
that she could see through the darkness;
that I could fall into those eyes
and just keep falling forever.

I hadn't known the gun was loaded.
I hadn't known how far I was from home.
I didn't believe I deserved it.
I didn't know what to do.

Trees lifted the moon into the sky.
In the moonlight, ordinary men
tore flesh from a broken corpse;
they grinned like dogs at a banquet.

No one explained this to me.
The woman sat beside me
singing of tea and oranges.
I wanted to slide into her.

I wanted her to kiss my wounds.
She kissed me on the mouth,
then blew the candle out
and left without another word.

Somebody cried, but it wasn't me.
Somebody burned the trees and the moon.
Somebody died of a dirty needle.
The dogs left nothing but bones.

What You Gave Me

for Jeff Apple

Even when we were nine,
you were what I wanted to be:
the brave one plunging into the creek's
green slime barefooted, catching snakes
barehanded with a careless skill
and courage I could only dream of.

I swam in your wake,
sat on the bench while you became
State Champ, watched you lift my weight
in solid iron as the years passed.

You bought the motorcycle,
always waited for the girls to call,
and the phone was always ringing.
I got the grades, but who puts grades
in the family den like trophies?
What teenaged girl ever yearned
to be kissed by a straight-A student?

Once, much later, we were twenty-two,
some girl you liked had dumped you.
We were sitting in your kitchen.
"I feel so blue," you said, "I wish
I knew a way to say it like you can."

I'd never realized you might envy me,
that being held back in school
had bothered you. Your silence

always seemed so strong,
not the cowed shyness of a boy
well-meaning grown-ups had convinced
that he was dumb.

Every time I get a student
who's a little slow with words,
I remember that you never seemed
to notice how I waded in the creek
with sneakers on, the snakes each time
somehow just barely out of reach,
that you knew but didn't care
I wet the bed till I was nearly twelve,

that kids who can't articulate the blues
are songbirds locked in small cages
alone in darkened rooms.

The Poet as Athlete

for Lou

One look at him induces adjectives:
gargantuan, Brobdingnagian, humongous;
what manatees might look like
if they put on clothes. Somewhere under
all that vast expanse like open ocean
must be something solid, but no imagination
could be vast enough to conjure even
flaccid muscles, bones like coral atolls
in that briny, rolling sea.

Against the tide of gravity, he struggles
to the podium like someone swimming,
takes a drink of water, and begins:
a poem about the powerful intoxication
of his first car, a poem about
the expectation of a first teenaged love,
a poem about a son he doesn't have.

Surely he must know what we are thinking.
Surely he must swim through every day
against a tide of gravity and ridicule,
but in a sure voice steady as the tides,
he draws us to the heart
of what we share.

Not one word about his own affliction.
Consider poetry, how good poems
offer us the world with eyes renewed.
Now see the swimmer I am watching:
all discipline, all muscle, lean and hard.

140

The Beech Tree

My neighbor leans across the fence
and gestures upward grandly, making
with his two arms a tiny human
imitation of a beech tree lifting
two hundred years of sprawling growth.
"Quite a tree you've got!" he says,
"By God, I wish I owned it."

But though it lives in my backyard,
this tree belongs to the squirrels
leaping branches just beyond my window.
"You'd like to catch us, but you can't,"
they seem to scold the tabby cat
that crouches daily with a patience
too dim to comprehend the squirrels
own this tree and will not fall.

It belongs to the robins that nested
last year in a high sheltered fork.

It belongs to the insects burrowing
beneath its aging bark like miners.

I'm just the janitor: raking leaves,
pruning limbs to keep them from collapsing
the garage roof next door or climbing
into bed beside my wife and me.

Possession is a curious thing:
some things are not for owning,
and I don't mind caring for a tree

141

that isn't mine. I take my pay
in April re-awakening and summer shade.
Just now, I'm watching snow
collecting in the upper branches,
waiting for the robins to come home.

The Heart of the Poem

Split the ribcage open
with a heavy-bladed knife,
a hatchet or an axe.
Be careful with an axe;
it can do more damage than you need.

Grasp the ribs and pry them back.
They won't want to give at first:
pull hard and steadily;
keep pulling till they snap.

Forget about the skin;
it'll tear when the ribs give way.

After that, it's easy:
push the other guts aside,
let your fingers dig until the heart
seats firmly in your palm
like a baseball or a grapefruit,
then jerk it out.

Get rid of it.
Sentiment's for suckers.
Give us poetry.

Appearances

The deceiver
slithers into its chair
and coils its heavy body
into a lump, its head raised
and weaving slowly over the desk,
the forked tongue darting
out of a kind of sleepy
half-smile, testing the air.
Another day.

Two signs hang on the wall:
"Right" and "Left."
The right sign hangs on the left;
the left one hangs on the right.
The mahogany desktop gleams
like the cold eyes of a snake.
Where are the mice?

A knock at the door:
an imperceptible flashing
of razored fangs.
"Come in," says the man
seated behind the desk,
"Tell me the nature of things."

Not Your Problem

Avoid this place.

Here time travels in tiny circles
like the hands of a clock.

Here dust rises like smoke
until it rains;
then we lie down in mud
and dream of dust.

Here our children will never learn
to read or write; their teeth
will rot from their heads;
they will join the army, or die
like us beneath bombs.

Here men with guns at night
make sleeping people in houses
disappear.

Here voters are branded with ink,
and those unmarked are found
days later in trash dumps.

Here being poor is a crime
unless we are also quiet;
almost everyone is poor,
and we can hear a bullet
being chambered a mile away.

145

We will change all this.

You won't want to be here
when we do.

The Way Light Bends

A kind of blindness, that's what's needed now.
Better not to know. Better to notice
the way light bends through trees in winter dusk.

What, after all, does knowledge bring? Cold rage,
the magnitude of history, despair.
A kind of blindness, that's what's needed now

because it's hard enough to pay the bills.
So long as you can still appreciate
the way light bends through trees in winter dusk,

what's possible, what is, what can't be changed
is better left to dreamers, fools, and God.
A kind of blindness, that's what's needed now,

the wisdom not to think about what waits
in dark holes beneath the earth. Marvel at
the way light bends through trees in winter dusk

and don't imagine how the light will bend
the way light bends through trees in winter dusk
and burst forever when the missiles fly.
A kind of blindness, that's what's needed now.

The Storm

Midnight, and a rain falls black,
October cold, the wind obstreperous,
stinging.
        You wait on the unlit
platform, soaked and shivering,
thinking the years at once
too far gone and far too many
to carry.
        At last, the last
train to anywhere comes
out of the darkness, your dark
wet coat too perfectly black
until the train is almost past:

the engineer brakes to a stop
far down the tracks.
The conductor opens the rear door,
motions for you to run.

But you are where you belong,
it is raining and cold,
and what is a world or a life
without principles?
        The engineer,
the conductor, are wrong.

You hold your ground. The conductor
signals the engineer, the train

hesitates,
        then moves on,
                leaving you
standing alone,
heart filled with obscenities
cold and black like the rain.

How I Live

for Leela
who gave me the first line

I bumped my head on the setting sun.
The night had only just begun
and I was dizzy already, reeling
like a drunk walking on the ceiling
of a world turned upside down.

A steady star burned above the town
I thought I lived in, but I couldn't
find it, and a voice said I shouldn't
even bother, what with the wind
rising, clouds piling, tide coming in.

What was I supposed to do?
Jump ship? Run amok in Fortescue?
Abandon, mother, wife and daughter
to the lunatics and pimps? Slaughter
common sense and go to sleep?

I couldn't stop thinking of the sheep,
the wolves, pigs, rifles, missiles
and a diesel east of Barstow, whistle
howling through the empty desert night
as if it were a soul in headlong flight.

Maybe I was only dreaming
all the lies, the calculated scheming,
computating, calibrating. Maybe not.
It never seems to end, I thought,

the dizziness, the mocking darkness.

Then an owl swooped low, the starkness
of its beating wings against the air
too savage, too beautiful to care.
Then a stillness, and a man alone
calling: Is it here? Is this my home?

The Children of Hanoi

June 1990

There in that place the Americans bombed,
where the children were sent to the hills
away from their mothers and fathers,
taking their laughter with them,
leaving their city in darkness,

in the market among the bicycles,
baskets of spices and fruit,
beer and cigarettes, burlap bags
and people singing their words
in a language forty centuries old,

in a toystore cluttered with orange
inflatable fish and wind-up monkeys
and dolls: two identical warplanes,
flight leader and wingman,
"U.S. Air Force" stenciled on the sides.

And the children touch them without fear,
pick them up with their hands,
put them into the sky
and pretend they are flying—
in their eyes, nothing but now.

Song for Leela, Bobby and Me

for Robert Ross

The day you flew to Tam Ky, I was green
with envy. Not that lifeless washed-out
green of sun-bleached dusty jungle utes.
I was rice shoot green, teenage green.
This wasn't going to be just one more
chickenscratch guerrilla fight:
farmers, women, boobytraps and snipers,
dead Marines, and not a Viet Cong in sight.
This was hardcore NVA, a regiment at least.
But someone had to stay behind,
man the bunker, plot the H&I.

I have friends who wonder why I can't
just let the past lie where it lies,
why I'm still so angry.
As if there's something wrong with me.
As if the life you might have lived
were just a fiction, just a dream.
As if those California dawns
were just as promising without you.
As if the rest of us can get along
just as well without you.

Since you've been gone, they've taken boys
like you and me and killed them in Grenada,
Lebanon, the Persian Gulf, and Panama.
And yet I'm told I'm living in the past.
Maybe that's the trouble: we're a nation
with no sense of history, no sense at all.

I still have that photo of you
standing by the bunker door, smiling shyly,
rifle, helmet, cigarette, green uniform
you hadn't been there long enough to fade
somewhere in an album I don't have
to look at any more. I already know
you just keep getting younger. In the middle
of this poem, my daughter woke up crying.
I lay down beside her, softly singing;
soon she drifted back to sleep.
But I kept singing anyway.
I wanted you to hear.

from
The Distance We Travel

How It All Comes Back

The bullet entered between the eyes,
a hole like a punctuation mark
from an AK-47 or M-16,
white at the edges but glistening black,
a tunnel straight to the brain.
That's what I saw when I picked her up

before crushed veins reopened, blood
began to cover my shirt, reflex
covered the hole with my hand,
and I started calling for help.

It was only a child's fall on a rock;
it only took three stitches to close,
but I couldn't look at my daughter
for months without seeing that hole:
I'd seen holes like that before,
but never on someone alive.

More Than You Ever Imagined

You wake to a pain in your right side,
the left shoulder always stiff,
knees aching. Age advances
one sore muscle at a time,
hair on the head of the face
in the mirror peppered with gray.
You still can't shave without bleeding.

On the radio news, nothing but war.
American planes are bombing Baghdad.
Knicked in three places, you remember
the nameless dead you carried home.
You remember you promised to bury them.
You thought you could. You didn't know
there'd be more than you ever imagined.

Guatemala

for Kari

Like a large cat rising out of a sleep
after a good kill is fully digested,
its stomach beginning to ask for more,
the General grins in the woman's face,
pulls the top of her dress aside,
cups a breast in his hand and pinches
the nipple hard, like a bullet.
She winces. American, twenty-six,
she's come to bring the joy of Jesus
to the children of the city dump:
thousands of families, thousands
of children, living on trash.
She runs a kitchen and school,
begs for what she gets and thanks
the Lord, but wants to know
why the General and his friends
feed steak to family dogs while
families starve. He rubs her breast.
He rubs his groin against her hip.
"There will always be poor," he says.
"The ones in the dump would find you.
Your embassy would send me a letter.
Nothing more would be done."

The Trouble with Poets

So after I had read my poems,
the man who'd promised two hundred dollars
"payable the night of the Poetry Reading"
gave me this soft-shoe song-and-dance shuffle
about hard times in Poetryville and a guy
named Dwight who'd split for DC
on short notice—and the short of it was
I only got eighty-five bucks.

If you owe the bank two hundred dollars
and you only pay them eighty-five,
two guys in trench coats and dark glasses
come and take your car away.

But I'm not the bank,
and this was only a bar in South Philadelphia.

I was just about to go away angry
when a man at the bar called me over.
"Hey, listen, Mac," he said, "People get
messed with and short-changed and fucked over,
glad-handed, back-handed, brass-knuckled,
bludgeoned, bullied, beat up and knocked down
day in and day out all over the world.
That's life, Mac. That's the trouble
with poets: you guys refuse
to accept it."

The Old Soldiers

The old soldiers imagine themselves warriors.
They remember the benediction of duty,
the future of women and pride.
They remember the beautiful weapons,
and always the beautiful dead.

They are wearing their colored ribbons.
They are watching the years march by.
They are full of a glorious sadness,
believing themselves important
and cheated of what they have earned.

The Lotus Cutters of Hô Tây

The lotus cutters gather morning
into their small reed boats.

Graceful as egrets, they weave
through mist so fine it curls

them into its gossamer arms
like a woman holding a child.

One turns to catch a ball
of sunshine balanced on a stalk.

Who would come ten thousand miles
to bomb them?

What have they ever done
but keep the sun from falling?

Making Love in the Garden

I have never seen you naked before.
Not like this: nothing at all
but sunlight, sky and skin
here in the garden
where you and your mother used to play,
the garden rapidly going to seed,
the house sold and awaiting settlement.

Nothing can bring your mother back.
Missing the ferry, losing the key,
up all night with intestinal flu,
getting a ticket while driving to see
your mother's grave for the last time:
God has been telling you all week long
what you remember is what you have.

That, and a garden empty of all but us.
The sun reflects the whiteness of skin,
the ocean breeze cool as grass,
two brown nipples, swaying breasts,
two white thighs across my hips,
hairs intertwined like the lives
that lie before us, yours and mine.

Once in awhile, love should be
with nothing between a man and a woman
and the universe they've chosen to share
but good clean air and no regrets,
your eyes half-closed,
the wetness of you,
pelvis a passionate blur.

Singing Hymns in Church

My mother loved to sing,
but couldn't sing to save her life.
My childhood passed from week to week,
counted out in Sunday mornings
I would have to sit beside her
in the first pew, pretending I was
far away and she was not my mother
while she bellowed out the hymns
so loud and badly I was sure
God or Mr. Hoot would silence her
with lightning or a sharp word
and look at me as if to say,
"Why don't you keep her quiet?"

At home, she couldn't sing out loud.
Her husband and her sons were quick
to say what God and Mr. Hoot
were too polite to tell her.
All those many hurts she carried
in the stillness of her heart
we never thought of, being men
too conscious only of ourselves,
too ignorant to understand the beauty
of the Christian Church where once a week
my mother sang for God and me,
and all the angels sang along,
and what she heard was joy.

Star Light, Star Bright

Under stars in late October cold
you asked, if stars are suns,
why is ours much bigger than the rest.
I said, because they're far away.
As far away as Grammy's house, you asked.
Farther still, I said, much farther.
Where is Grammy now, you asked.
Her body's in the ground, I said,
but maybe what she really was
is up there somewhere shining down
like starlight you and I can feel
all around us on a night like this.
You stood in silence for awhile,
gazing up, one thoughtful hand
resting lightly on my shoulder,
one stretched out and turned palm up
as if to catch the starlight.
Then you said, almost singing,
        what a pretty feeling
        to be a little star,
        white, and beautiful.
I could feel the whole heart of you
lifting dreams beyond the reach
of earthbound limitations and I
love you more than you will know
until I'm starlight and you understand
how each of us needs little stars
to lift our dreams beyond ourselves,
and I was hers, and you were mine.

Finding My Old Battalion
Command Post

What we came here to find
was never ours. After the miles
we've traveled, after the years
we've dreamed if only we could touch
the wound again, we could be whole,
no small wonder to discover
only a lethal past between us,
what we thought a brotherhood
only a mutual recollection of fear.

Something was lost, but it wasn't ours,
and if not here, we'd only have lost it
somewhere else. The young always do.
That is why we remember the young
who die too soon to lose
anything but their lives.
That is why we envy them.
They will always believe the world
is simple, and they only die once.

This is not what I intended,
but it won't stay down: nobody
wants a fool for a lover, a fool
for a father, a foolish friend.
Nobody wants excuses. Still,
there are stars that burn with no light;
there are things too evil for words,
too evil for silence.
Even a fool needs a friend.

But only the dead are permanent,
so we've come to this place to find—
what? Lost innocence? Our true selves?
What we think we were before we learned
to recognize incoming enemy mortars
in our sleep? What you've found is just
how frail I am. Now you think I can't
be trusted to my buttons. Grunt to grunt,
you say, it's all that matters.

Nevermind particulars. This is just
between the two of us: "Heave ho,
into the lake you go with all
the other alewife scuz and foamy
harbor scum. But isn't it a pity."
Yes, a pity, though I've long since learned
that losses are the way things are.
And look, I've found a village where I once
thought nothing green would ever grow.

Sleeping with General Chi

The old general wants me to sleep.
He pats the bed and points to my shoes.
His voice tells me this is a man
accustomed to being obeyed.

After the ride to Tay Ninh
in a sheetmetal box with two flat tires,
the red laterite dust in our lungs
so thick you could hear it bubble,

after the commissar's welcoming speech:
so many wounded, so many homeless,
so many dead—even the general
falling asleep in his chair,

I wanted to walk to the river
to sit in the shade and wash my lungs
with the cool breath of a graceful land
of buffalo boys and herons,

but the guard at the gate spoke
only Vietnamese, and I did not.
Only a boy, he held his weapon
at port arms and tried to smile.

Years ago, in another life,
I had killed young men like him
and they had tried to kill me.
But not today. I'm tired of fighting.

So I turned away and found
the general under a fan in tropical heat.
I want to explain what's happened,
but the general wants me to sleep.

I've never slept with a general before.
Men don't sleep with their officers
and don't take naps together in bed
in the afternoon in my country.

But this is not my country.
The general pats my arm and dozes off,
serene as any aging man content
to have his grandchild sleeping near.

For a Coming Extinction

Vietnam. Not a day goes by
without that word on my lips.
I hear the rattle of small-arms fire
when I tuck my daughter in,
think of the stillborn dreams of other men
when I make love to my wife,
sharp snap of a flag in high wind—
blood, stars, an ocean of ignorance.
Sometimes I mumble the word to myself
like a bad dream, or a prayer:
Vietnam, Vietnam. Already
it's become what it never was:
heroic, a noble cause. Opportunity
squandered, chance to learn turned
inside out by cheap politicians
and *China Beach*. So many so eager
so soon for others to die,
and the time's fast arriving
when Vietnam means only a distant
spot on the globe, only a name
on a dusty map, when no one alive
will understand what was or is,
what might have been and was lost.

After the Latest Victory

I call the sea. The wind calls back.
No seagulls' cries, no sailors' ghosts,
not mermaids, God, nor any human voice
disturbs the silence closing hard behind
the last reverberations of that solitary cry.

Does sound just die? Or does the universe
reverberate with cries from Planet Earth?
Novenas, speeches, shouts, whole supplications
striking Jupiter, careening off the stars
like frozen screams or unsaid thoughts?

Only the wind, and the waves' dull roar,
the dune grass dancing for the moon.
Behind me lies a continent asleep,
drunk with martial glory and an empire's pride,
though each is transient as sand.

This continent was called the New Jerusalem.
So much hope and expectation carried
in the hearts of men and women brave
enough to hazard all in search of this.
Look what we have made of it.

In Fairmount Park, a girl is raped.
Her father is a soldier in the Middle East.
Her brother cannot read or write.
The rapist wants a pair of sneakers
like the ones he's seen in Reebok ads.

The moon's wide river rides the swells

171

from breakers to the dark horizon.
Above me, like a dignified procession,
the stars turn slowly through the night,
indifferent to our helplessness.

Guns

Again we pass that field
green artillery piece squatting
by the Legion Post on Chelten Avenue,
its ugly little pointed snout
ranged against my daughter's school.

"Did you ever use a gun
like that?" my daughter asks,
and I say, "No, but others did.
I used a smaller gun. A rifle."
She knows I've been to war.

"That's dumb," she says,
and I say, "Yes," and nod
because it was, and nod again
because she doesn't know.
How do you tell a four-year-old

what steel can do to flesh?
How vivid do you dare to get?
How explain a world where men
kill other men deliberately
and call it love of country?

Just eighteen, I killed
a ten-year-old. I didn't know.
He spins across the marketplace
all shattered chest, all eyes and arms.
Do I tell her that? Not yet,

though one day I will have
no choice except to tell her
or to send her into the world
wide-eyed and ignorant.
The boy spins across the years

till he lands in a heap
in another war in another place
where yet another generation
is rudely about to discover
what their fathers never told them.

The Distance We Travel

The strange American steps out of the night
into the flickering light of candles and small
fires and open stoves cooking evening meals,
families and neighbors clustered together,
moving like birds on the wings of words.

Discreetly their eyes follow the man,
bowls and chopsticks rising, pausing,
gracefully rising, so subtle a gesture
he wonders if he has imagined it.

In silence he passes among them
nodding agreeably, nodding in wonder,
nodding at what he remembers was here,
wanting to gather the heart of this place
into himself, to make it forgive him.

He is sure the older faces remember:
"Why are you here? Who are you?"
Questions alive in thick summer air,
a suggestion of posture.

But he has no answers to give them.
His explanation lies on his tongue
like a bird with a broken wing.
Only the fact of the lives around him.
Only the need to be near.

Two girls too young to remember
are playing badminton without a net.

They turn to look, then giggle and stop.
One offers a raquet and shuttlecock.

In the dim street, he begins to play.
He marvels at his ineptitude,
their simple delight with his laughter,
how they have taken him into their game
as if he were not a stranger.

From out of the shadows a stool appears,
a cool drink. The girls' mother gestures
for him to sit. Unsure of himself,
he takes from his wallet a photograph.

"My daughter," he says, "Li-La."
He touches his heart with his open hand.
He writes the name in Vietnamese.
She touches the picture. The father appears,
another daughter, a nephew and son.

The father is reticent. Finally the stranger
touches the scars on his neck and says, "VC."
He points to the opposite bank of the river.
"Over there," he says, "*Tet Mau Than.*"

The father lifts his shirt to reveal
a scar on his chest. "VC," he says, then
drops his shirt and lights a cigarette,
offers one to the stranger. Together
they smoke the quiet smoke of memory.

Seven years the father spent in a camp
for prisoners of war. The wife
lightly touches her husband's knee.
Lightly his hand goes to hers.

The stranger considers the years he has spent
wearing the weight of what he has done,
thinking his tiny part important.
The father points to the gap-toothed bridge
the VC dropped in the river, long repaired.

The children are playing badminton again.
The shuttlecock lands in the stranger's lap.
"Li-La," the father softly says, touching
the stranger's heart with his open hand.

Mostly Nothing Happens

Mostly Nothing Happens

East Mt. Airy,
Philadelphia

Walking home on Upsal Street,
I saw a group of young black men
gathered on the sidewalk up ahead.
What now, I thought, heartbeat
rising in a heartbeat, eyes
instantly attempting to assess
intentions, weapons, routes of egress,
*do I just keep walking, do I
take a detour to avoid them, if I—*
Shame arrived before an answer:
what would Harris think, I thought,
*what would Harris think of me
for fearing who when we were young
was him?*

Harris's girlfriend was pregnant
when we were young, and every night
the two of us would read her letters,
flashlights pressed against the floor.
God help us if our drill instructors
caught us, but gentleness was rare
and we were very much in need
of gentleness on Parris Island,
so together we would read
those gentle letters.

She'd write about the baby's kicking,
how she'd guess what sex it was,

and if it was a boy they'd name him John.
"That's my name," he'd say each time.
"I know," I'd say, too embarrassed
to admit I didn't know a thing.
I'd touched a girl's secrets only twice,
and only with my hand,
and here's a guy who's really done it—
done it and she's pregnant, and he's
neither married nor abandoned her!

All of this a wonder to a small town kid
who'd never heard sex talked about
in proper conversation, get a girl pregnant
and you marry her, no questions, no debate.
Furthermore, a town where Negroes didn't live,
and terms like jungle bunny, nigger, coon,
if seldom heard in proper conversation,
were seldom far from lips.

But I was scared to death
of drill instructors huge as houses,
mean as pit bulls, psychopathic maniacs
out to keep the Viet Cong from killing me
by killing me themselves, or so I thought.
Who at seventeen could understand
how terrifying war would be,
how much more obscene? This place
was worse than any place I'd ever been.
I thought I'd never leave alive.

To my surprise, so did Harris.
Urban, street-smart, soon-to-be-a-father

Harris, just as scared as I was.
And his voice so soft, his hand
upon my wrist when we were reading
softer still, a heart so big
I thought that mine would burst.
Through all those lonely southern nights,
through all that frightened Carolina summer,
those two boys from Perkasie and Baltimore
stuck together and survived.

Harris is the reason why I'm here:
I chose an integrated neighborhood
because I didn't want a child of mine
to reach the age of seventeen
with no one in her life
who isn't white.

But something isn't working right:
the neighborhood's got crack cocaine
and dirty needles lying in the gutter,
muggings, robberies, burglaries,
guns more prevalent than basketballs
and people willing to use them.
Two teenaged kids, a couple on a date,
were shot two blocks from here
for two dollars, and just last week
a man was taken from his car
at gunpoint, shot, and left for dead
a football field's length from my front door.
How much longer will it be before
the victim's me, my wife or daughter?
And if and when it happens,
odds are high the perpetrator's
going to be a young black man.

I hate to say those words out loud.
I hate the world that's made them true.
I hate distrusting men
before I even know their names, and so
I chose to trust those men on Upsal Street,
and this time got away with it.
But every time I trust a stranger
just might be the time I'm wrong.
What then?

What would Harris do, I thought,
what would Harris tell me I should do?
Why not find him? Why not ask?

You'd think it would be hard to find a friend
you haven't seen in twenty-seven years,
but I found him faster than I ever dreamed
or ever cared to: Panel 26E, Line 105.
John Lee Harris, Jr., born September 12th, 1947,
killed in Vietnam September 21st, 1967.

Damn.

You'd think that on the day he died,
an angel might have come to me.
A heron, or a raven.
But no. Only the day came
and went away again like other days
in Vietnam, and then my tiny piece of that
obscenity was over, so I thought,
and I too went away, wanting to forget.

I didn't think of Harris for a long time,
but I never forgot what he taught me,

and now I want to pound my fists
against that stupid granite wall:
"Come out of there, John Harris!
I need to know if what I am is cautious
or hysterical, a realist or just a racist,
how the world is, how am I to live in it.
I need answers," but instead
I get that war again,
still taking friends and giving only
wounds that never heal.

And now I've got this other war as well.
Last summer someone tried to force
my daughter's bedroom window open.
This was on a Tuesday afternoon.
Did Harris and his girlfriend ever marry?
Did they have a son and name him John?
Or did they have, like me, a baby girl?
And did he get to hold his child
and wonder at the tiny life he'd made
before he went away and died, fighting
yellow people in a white man's war?
Would he understand I'm not afraid for me?

That son of his would be a man
about the age of the men I passed
on Upsal Street last week,
the pounding in my chest so loud,
surely they could hear it.
I don't want to leave this neighborhood.
I want to think we'll be okay
if only we can touch the best
in others and ourselves.
I still don't keep a gun around

because I'm through with guns,
but every day is like a day at war:
mostly nothing happens,
but you never know what's waiting
when or where or how.
The first black friend I ever had
died one day when something happened.
Every day I'm always on patrol.

Poems Not Included in
Previous Collections

Lost Years

I still remember bicycle rides
along the Susquehanna: me on the bar
on a pillow, holding tight, you peddling,
John and Bob just old enough to ride
on their own. We were a family then.
I even remember you singing me to sleep.

None of the years between
matter now. Now I love you
as I did then: fiercely, from the gut,
without having to pause first and think,
without the confusion of all those times
one of us failed—you, or I—whatever it was

that drove us apart but kept us
paired like clumsy dancers at a prom,
at arms' length, ill at ease. Lost years

are better forgotten.
You are here now. In a hospital bed.
Hooked up to a tangle of wires and tubes.
I remember the feel of your hands
on the handlebar, the gurgle of moving water,
the old rusting steamshovel at Red Rock.

I am singing a song
you taught me.

Secrets

Each room except the room you're in
is empty. No need to check.
How many times in forty-five years
did you wish for such a silence,
just a moment to collect yourself
amid the chaos of a life too full
with other people's needs?

And now you've got more silence
than you'll ever need, more time
than anyone should ever have
alone, each memory another moment
in a world where time holds
nothing but the past
and someone else's future.

What do you dream of?
What do you fear each time
you turn to hear Dad stirring
and you realize that what you hear
is just the silence of an empty house,
an absence permanent as stone?

Surely such a silence turns
the heart back in upon itself.
Do you find your husband there?
Four sons and four grandchildren?
Some little Brooklyn girl
in pigtails skipping rope
that once was you?

Mother, does it all come down
to empty rooms and half-imagined sounds
of someone familiar? So many hopes
and disappointments make a life.
What were yours? I'd like to know.

The Simple Lives of Cats

Cold spring rain drums hollow rhythms
on the windowpanes. Two a.m. The house
so dark and empty even the kittens
lie mesmerized by the echoing patter,
heads raised, ears twitching, eyes wide,
tiny noses sniffing the air for danger.

But the only danger here is me.
Once again I've lost it, temper flaring,
patience at a too-quick end, my daughter
crying, and my wife's heart sinking
in the sadness of another good day gone bad.
If sorry has a name, it must be mine.

The kittens don't suspect a thing.
One turns her head to lick my hand.
The other, having satisfied herself
this new sound filling up the night
is just another harmless curiosity,
stirs once, then settles in my lap.

Tonight my wife and child are sleeping
somewhere else. I've done this to myself
often enough to wonder just how many
chances I've got left. I stroke the cats,
who purr like engines; happy to be near,
they see no need for my improvement.

A Vietnamese Bidding Farewell
to the Remains of an American

Was your plane on fire, or did you die
of bullet wounds, or fall down exhausted?
Just so you died in the forest, alone.

Only the two of us, a woodcutter and his wife,
dug this grave for you, burned joss sticks,
prayed for you to rest in peace.

How could we know there'd be such a meeting,
you and I, once separated by an ocean,
by the color of our skin, by language?

But destiny bound our lives together.
And today, by destiny's grace,
you are finally going home.

I believe your American sky
is as blue as the sky above this country
where you've rested twenty years.

Is it too late to love each other?
Between us now, the ocean seems so small.
How close are our two continents.

I wish a tranquil heaven for your soul,
gemmed with twinkling stars and shining moon.
May you rest forever in the soil of your home.

[From the original Vietnamese poem by Tran Thi My Nhung,
translated by Phan Thao Chi and adapted by W. D. Ehrhart.]

America in the Late 20th Century

He's giving up his paper route.
Only ten, and here he's written up
already in the Boston *Globe*:
held hostage by a customer who
shot him with a bow and arrow.
A hunting arrow, for Chrissake,
the steel sharp tip meant to kill.

What would cause a man to shoot
a boy like that? Ten years old.
Innocent enough to want to work
instead of splitting people's heads
or lifting people's wallets.
I used to carry papers as a kid.
No one ever took a shot at me.

I broke the Van Leer's window
once, put the Wilson's Wednesday
late edition through their door.
Neither family even made me pay.
I didn't like the Morgan's dog
or Jimmy Whiteneck, but the things
I feared a kid should rightly fear.

These days a kid must learn to fear
crazed customers with hunting bows
and random gunfire in the street
that killed a boy six blocks from here.
What an age to come of age:
better to sell cocaine than news—
fewer surprises, and you die rich.

194

The Open Door

The door was opened just enough
to let the wind inside the house
and curl itself from room to room
like mist, or like a bony finger calling:
Here. Come here. I've come for you.

I didn't even know the door was open
till I felt those quiet words, a tingling
in my spine, like flakes of ice on bare skin.
I shivered once, twice, turned, saw nothing
but a fleeting shadow and the door ajar.

So, I thought, and listened hard.
The old house groaned, as old houses do.
No other sound disturbed the night.
And yet I'd seen a shadow, and a chill
settled on my heart and softly shook it.

Afraid, I tiptoed to my daughter's room,
but she was sleeping, and the cat beside her
didn't stir. Down the hall, my wife slept too.
I checked each room, each closet, the attic
and the basement. Nothing was amiss.

Sleep, I thought, but I couldn't sleep.
I hadn't left the door ajar. I know
I saw a shadow, just a passing breath
but real as cold or love or sorrow
or the loss of dreams we hold too dear.

What I Know About Myself

for Gloria Emerson

I always have to wash my hands
before my wife and I make love.
She likes the feel of clean hands
and I the feel of soapy hands,
so warm, so slick, so like
the secret places that we'll
soon be sharing.

A friend told me a story once
about a woman who planted a bomb
in a French café in Algiers.
The woman, Algerian, hadn't wanted
to do it. The men had told her
she must, it was her duty.
A hand, a French woman's hand,
had landed at her feet.

"Men," my friend had said, "love war.
Women endure it, but men love it.
You were there. You know.
Say you deny it, I don't care."

She reached for a book of photographs
from Vietnam. She'd been there, too.
"Look at the woman's face," she said,
"Look at them all. Those women
never looked at you. How could they
look at men with rifles
pointing at them? Look how young

196

you are. How innocent. How evil."

She knew I knew what she meant,
and she was right.
"Our hands will never be clean,"
she said, "but we must try."

And so I do, washing my hands
again and again of the filth
I've touched and never want
to touch my wife.
I want clean hands
to make her sigh and spread
and share those secret places
what I know about myself
can't find.

The Last Time I Dreamed
About the War

Ruth and I were sitting in the kitchen
ten years after Vietnam. She was six-feet-two
and carried every inch of it with style,
didn't care a fig that I was seven
inches shorter. "You've got seven inches
where it counts," she'd laugh, then lift her chin
and smile as if the sun had just come out.

But she didn't want to hear about the war.
I heard the sound of breaking glass
coming from my bedroom, went to look:
VC rats were jumping through the window.
They looked like rats, but they were Viet Cong.
Don't ask me how I knew. You don't forget
what tried to kill you.

I tried to tell her, but she wouldn't listen.
"Now look, Ruth!" I said so loud the woman
sleeping next to me woke up and did
what Ruthie in my dream refused to do:
she listened to me call the name
of someone she had never heard of,
anger in my voice, my body hard.

The woman I was sleeping with
would be my wife, but wasn't yet. I was
still a stranger with a stranger's secrets
and a tattoo on my arm. She'd never known a man
who'd fought in Vietnam, put naked women on

the wall, smoked marijuana, drank whiskey straight.
And here I was in bed with her,
calling someone else's name in anger.

She wanted to run, she told me later,
but she didn't. She married me instead.
Don't ask me why. I only know
you never know what's going to save you
and I've never dreamed again about the war.

New Poems

Purple Heart

for Dave Connolly

The wraith of a shadow shivered the air
the way whatever was green around us
always went silent
just before the bullets arrived.

I never got used to the terror
of sudden beginnings
or sudden conclusions,
the random ways people die,
so I knew what I felt this afternoon
was a fact.
And I knew what was coming.

But this time nothing happened.
Only that barely perceptible shiver,
and the world going on as before.

Spooky, I thought.
Then Lisa called
to tell me you'd had a heart attack.

Which of us could have imagined
middle-aged men with failing hearts
when we were young and strong and afraid
to imagine we'd see tomorrow?
Who could have told us
the terrors still to come?

But the shiver I felt was no coincidence.

Rise from your bed and live, my friend,
for the world is still a dangerous place
and I need the few friends I can trust.

Red-tailed Hawks

Mill Grove
Audubon, Pennsylvania

These chattering children fill the woods
with so much raw exuberance one wonders
what's the point of coming here
when any local playground would suffice.

Their teacher twice tells Michael and James,
"Don't throw acorns, please," to no effect:
they start again the moment she turns
to remind Adrienne, "Stay on the path."

Leela's worried she'll fall in the creek.
Chelsea and Ben are pushing each other
when someone, one of the children, shouts,
"There's a hawk!" and points.

"There's another!" "There!" "Another!"
other children cry: four red-tailed hawks
lazily circling, gliding, whirling, wheeling,
riding an unseen thermal up so high

the children tip their heads straight back
and still the hawks rise higher, higher still,
until they're only four black dots
of elemental joy against white clouds,

the children, even Michael and James,
so intent, so silent one can almost hear
wings they want to lift them
where the hawks have gone.

Beautiful Wreckage

What if I didn't shoot the old lady
running away from our patrol,
or the old man in the back of the head,
or the boy in the marketplace?

Or what if the boy—but he didn't
have a grenade, and the woman in Hue
didn't lie in the rain in a mortar pit
with seven Marines just for food,

Gaffney didn't get hit in the knee,
Ames didn't die in the river, Ski
didn't die in a medevac chopper
between Con Thien and Da Nang.

In Vietnamese, Con Thien means
place of angels. What if it really was
instead of the place of rotting sandbags,
incoming heavy artillery, rats and mud.

What if the angels were Ames and Ski,
or the lady, the man, and the boy,
and they lifted Gaffney out of the mud
and healed his shattered knee?

What if none of it happened the way I said?
Would it all be a lie?
Would the wreckage be suddenly beautiful?
Would the dead rise up and walk?

Strangers

In the photograph, my mother's slim,
almost petite. Her white dress
reaches barely to her knees, revealing
slender legs on white high heels.
My father wears a three-piece suit,
dark brown or blue, dark tie, white shirt,
dark shoes with white tops, 1940s-style.
Each with an arm around the other's back,
they face the camera, and they're smiling.

She's twenty-three, he's twenty-four,
and nothing in the photograph suggests
that by the time they reach the age
that I am as I sit here staring
at the two of them together,
she'll be sliding toward obesity,
a sad and stoic woman married
to a man who's burning slowly inward
like a star collapsing on itself
for reasons neither he nor she nor
all the well-intentioned doctors
who applied electrodes to his brain
and took his money in exchange for drugs
ever did explain or ever could.

I stare and stare, trying to remember,
but the people in this photograph
are strangers. Nothing looks familiar
but the fraying, ragged edges
of the paper, and the crack that seems
to tear them both apart.

Not for You

The man with your name and your life
isn't you.
                    Well, yes, it's your name,
and yes it's your life, okay,
but he can't be you.
                    His hair's turning gray,
his wife's turning the corner on her way to work,
and he's going nowhere.
                    Not
in all your nightmares did you ever imagine
you would come to this: a small life,
a few friends, a lot of dreams
that came and went: an ordinary life.

You always knew an ordinary life
wasn't for you.

Oh, not for you with the wind
at your heart and the ache in your soul
about to take wing like a bird.

This can't be you.   There's some mistake.

Prayer for My Enemies

> "Love thine enemies."
> —Jesus of Nazareth

Because I love you, I wish for you
to listen all your waking hours to homilies
and sermons by the Pope, and when you sleep,
to sleep with the smell of rendering plants
stuffing your nostrils until you puke.
May your car keys and credits cards
come to the hands of unscrupulous teens
who know your street, the house where you live.
May your lights go out on Broadway,
may your toilets forever be clogged,
may all your vegetables be overcooked.

You think it's a joke, but it's not.
Because I love you, I wish for you
an end to all that's good in your life,
each little thing, no matter how small,
how seemingly simple or unimportant.
May your every moment become a desert
and everyone you care about fall silent.
May even the earth refuse your body,
may large animals tear your flesh,
may the buzzards pick your carcass clean,
scatter your bones to the wind.

Suffer the Little Children

Oh, how we wanted to be good.
We brought our nickels every week, our
pennies earned collecting bottles,
doing chores, and put them in the jar.
We were saving for a heifer

for a village in darkest Africa.
We didn't know where Africa was,
but lions and gorillas lived in Africa,
and Mrs. Kugler told us Jesus
loved the little children of the world,

and there were children in this village.
In slides that Mrs. Kugler showed,
the Africans were singing in a crude
bare church of grass and local timber
with a plain wooden cross for a steeple

while a missionary family beamed.
But the Africans were very poor,
their children needed milk, and only
we, the six-year-olds of Mrs. Kugler's
Sunday School class in Lewisburg in 1954,

could help them. We could save them.
We could buy a heifer for their village
if only we could fill the heifer jar.
But the jar was big, our coins so small,
and as the weeks and months passed by,

it seemed we'd never fill that jar.
We were six years old, the fate of Africa
was in our hands, the weight of it so heavy,
but we didn't want to disappoint
our teacher, or the Africans, or Jesus.

Dropping Leela Off at School

My daughter's reached an age
where daddy kissing her
in public just won't do.
In second grade, she's too
self-conscious, too grown up.
And so I only watch
her run across the play-
ground, leap a wall, top a
hill to stand triumphant
in her independence.

But as I turn to go,
she glances quickly left
and right to see who's there,
raises hand to lips, and
quickly throws a kiss a-
cross the space between us,
as if to say she knows
already just how hard
the world can be, how hard
it is, how little she
enjoys pretending
not to need me.

After the Winter of 1994

When the first storm struck, we didn't complain.
We thought: *Okay, we can handle this.*
It's winter. You shovel. It's no big deal.
But the second storm brought freezing rain,
leaving four inches of glittering ice
snapping trees, dropping wires,
paralyzing the world. The third storm
covered the ice with thirteen inches of snow,
then the fourth storm dumped more ice,
and as pipes burst and furnaces failed,
we dug through the attic for extra clothes
and swore we would never survive.
By the time the fifth storm hit, our minds
were as empty as rooms in a house
for sale, our hearts bereft of even
the memory of hope, refusing to quit
only for reasons we couldn't explain.

When the first snowdrops popped from the earth,
we didn't believe them, didn't believe
the crocuses. "This won't last," we said,
and knowingly nodded, hunkering down
to receive whatever was coming.
But the dogwoods bloomed, the azaleas
started to bud, and the grass and trees
turned that exuberant shade of green
that proclaims the arrival of spring
no matter what winter has tried to do
to eradicate joy from the world.
All day we've bathed in the warmth of the sun

and tonight we swim through a river of dreams,
the moon alive, the forsythias
glowing with ambient light so yellow
it almost hurts our eyes—but don't for a
moment think we're complaining. Not us.

Drought

Perkasie, Pennsylvania, 1957

I had never before seen anything die.
Maybe a squirrel struck by a car,
or a bird caught by a cat, but nothing
so vivid, so slow, so thorough as this,

so little changing from day to day
we hardly noticed the thickening
algae, the yellowy-green of it sick
for weeks with the absence of water,

till we suddenly found ourselves walking
where always only water ever had been.
Only the holes held water now, and the holes
grew smaller, the holes grew crowded,

the fish grew frantic until they could
only lie on their sides in the mud
gulping at water that wasn't there,
and even the mud in the deepest holes

would be brittle tomorrow, the fish
encrusted with blue bottle flies, each fly
as big as a thumbnail, hungry, the only
sounds our feet on the creek bed snapping

like rivets in iron heat, and the buzzsaw
buzzing of tens of thousands of flies
feasting on death, even our memories
of water too cruel to be spoken aloud.

Variations on Squam Lake

I

Night comes down to a loon calling
and finds two herons at water's edge,
the lake so still, the stars fall in,
the trees bend down and scoop them out,
lift them back to the sky.

II

Night comes down to a loon calling
and finds an errant star falling

into a lake so still it seems
made only of gossamer dreams

until a great blue heron's wake
disturbs the surface of the lake

for a moment or two before
the stillness settles in once more

and the moon rises and the loon
calls out again, greeting the moon.

The Perversion of Faith

Saigon/HCMC
June 1990

The riverside banquet, extravagance
served by women in flowing *ao dais*,
might be explained as a lapse in judgment,
a clumsy desire to please and impress,

but the women were no mistake:
young enough to be our daughters,
girls procured by a former Viet Cong.
One took my hand and placed it on her lap.

I thought of an evening years before,
of a frail old soldier, Mr. Giai,
and of what the war had cost him:
thirty years, three fingers, his oldest son.

I thought of how the Saigon River
so serenely slapped the pilings, how
his voice had sounded like a tiny bird
beating back a sadness with its wings.

Mr. Giai has once met Ho Chi Minh.

The First French Kiss

I've forgotten the pain
of being fifteen and alone
with fiery-haired Ann Broderick,
girl I'd adored all year,
who suddenly found me attractive
in the back seat of Max Hunsicker's car
parked in a lane off Hilltown Pike,
me with mush for a brain and a heart
beating to bust my ribs.

I've forgotten how we came
to an end because I couldn't
stop asking myself why
she wanted me now
when not before,
me the same kid as before:
taller, thinner, more
a young man than a boy,
but the same kid still
in the place where the pain lives.

But I've forgotten all that.
I've forgotten everything
except the way her tongue was in my mouth,
the warmth of it, the wetness of it,
promise of what I hardly dared
imagine, the woman's smell of her,
me with my too tight jeans
and my hands in all that hair.

Visiting My Parents' Grave

If you had told me thirty years ago
I'd miss this town, I'd have told you
—well, you know what I'd have said,
so smug it was, so self-content,
its point of view so narrow one could
get a better field of vision peering
through the barrel of a shotgun.
I, at seventeen, could see that much
and so much more I couldn't wait
to leave. It didn't help, of course,
that I was who I was:
the preacher's and the teacher's son,
blow my nose the whole town knew,
anonymous a word I used
to stare at in the dictionary,
wishing it were me. Yet here I am,
thirty years later, back again.

I've come at night because I know
in daylight I could walk these streets
from dawn to dusk, meeting no one
who would know my name, or even yours.
Peter Shelly's house lies buried under
Nockamixon Lake, the Bryan's dairy farm's
a shopping mall, tract housing's crowded
out the sledding run near Callowhill;
Jeff Apple's gone to Melbourne Beach,
Larry Rush went schizophrenic
paranoid, and just about the only
thing that hasn't changed is Larry's mom,

who's still convinced he'll come out right
if only he'll repent and turn to God.

Me, I'm pretty well convinced that she's
the reason Larry's nuts, but that's
the only thing I'm sure of anymore.
I've been to the other side of world,
said what I've thought, hedged no bets, had
no use for comfortable hypocrisies
or delicate interpretations
meant to keep the world the way it is.
I've quit every job I've ever had
for something else, for this or that, or else
because someone's always screwing someone
else, and silence to injustice
large or small is simply cowardice.

Which may be true, but what I've got
for all my years is unemployed
and unemployable, a dozen books
that no one reads, a wife who works
to earn what I cannot, a daughter
I have trouble looking in the eye
because I fear she'll recognize
her father for the failure he's become.
That's the worst of it: I don't trust
my own judgment anymore. What used
to seem so obvious has vanished
in the glare of consequences
prudent people manage to avoid.

So here I am: sitting on your gravestone
on a hill above this town I couldn't
wait to get as far away from
as the moon, and though I know it's only

an illusion, here's the moon just rising
over Skyline Drive so huge it looks
as if I'd only need to reach
my fingers out to touch it,
just like sitting here at night
makes the town appear like nothing's changed,
as if at any moment Jeff and Larry
might appear on bikes, wave to me, and shout,
"Let's chase the cows at Bryan's farm!"
As if the years might fall away
and let me start again.

Nothing Profound

If you need a reason to care,
consider this feather I've found,
consider the sweetness of bare
young arms in sunlight, or the round
perfection of a ripe pear.

Cycling the Rosental

for Adi Wimmer

The River Drau flows swiftly here,
and cold, and such a pale green
it whispers in a waking dream
we pedal through beneath the near

and jagged Slovene Alps, "Let go
of all that troubles you—believe
in all the world can be—I'll weave
a little spell to let you know

the song I sing is meant for you."
So it is, and so the flowers
also sing through all the hours
we ride together, sky so blue

we finally have to stop and strip,
jumping into the River Drau
like a couple of kids. And how
the icy pale water grips

us till our hearts cry out in pain
or joy, my friend, I don't know which,
nor does it matter: even if
we never pass this way again,

we'll know the river's always here,
these mountains, and the sky above
the Valley of Roses, and the love
that makes a day like this so dear.

223

Rehoboth, One Last Time

for Patty

I might have known trouble was coming.
How we kept it up through all these years.
How each summer but the one I spent at sea
I'd never miss the chance to visit,
even the year I had to drive
nonstop all night through driving rain.
How the moon would rise above those old
concrete submarine towers by the beach,
the moon's wide river spreading flames
across the darkness of Rehoboth Bay.
How our families grew around us.

But I might have known trouble was coming.
That last sad visit to Rehoboth Bay
everything had changed: all day those ugly
little jet skis whined like manic gnats,
and every night blaring music boomed
from newly-built nightclubs by the beach,
and I remember thinking how there's
not a place on earth so beautiful
people won't destroy it for a buck.
The day we left, I knew we'd never
be together here again. Not here,

though surely somewhere, I assumed
until your letter came, explaining
John had left you after twenty-two years.
So there you are, alone in Seaford,
you with your two teenaged daughters,

and your parttime job, and the wreckage
of the life you thought you still had coming
while John's vacationing this summer
with a woman half your age in Rome.
Just so, the things we love are lost
in ways we understand, and ways we don't.

What Goes Around Comes Around

to my oldest brother

Okay, our father was a shit.
Reverend John, the darling of Perkasie,
much beloved, quick with a joke, a kind word,
time for someone else's problems.

Never time for ours, of course, though no one
ever saw that side of him but us:
the man with nothing but ugly words
or none at all for days on end,

so full of rage at God-knows-what,
so full of guilt, so self-absorbed
four sons grew up beneath his roof
without his ever knowing who we were.

So he wasn't Robert Young, okay?
In the end, at least he understood
he'd blown it. Ponder this: your own father
asks for your forgiveness on his deathbed

and you turn your back and walk away.
And now you've got a son who's stolen,
lied, and flunked his way through adolescence
while you've been making piles of money

and spending it on courting women
from Maine to Moscow; a kid who should have
gone to Harvard pumping gas instead.
You think you're not responsible for that?

Maybe not, but when it's you
with no time left except to ask
forgiveness for the man you've been,
I wonder what your son will say to you.

The Sergeant

Alongapo, The Philippines, 1968

At night in the Seven-Eleven Club,
you watch the sailors dressed in white
fresh from the waters off Vietnam
get fleeced by the hostesses, brown
sensuous girls who dance with the sailors
for drinks containing no alcohol.

The girls can dance all night and never
get drunk, and at closing time the sailors,
who think they're about to get laid, get
shown the door and stagger back to their ships.

What do they know about loneliness,
those beautiful sailors in white,
sitting on ships on the blue beautiful sea,
launching beautiful bombers
into the beautiful sky,
firing beautiful five-inch projectiles
at places and people they'll never see.

In the morning you wake to a shabby
room in a cheap hotel with a hostess
who's charged you nothing but love,
the war in Asia, a war in America,
you in the middle, twenty years old,
cupping the breast of the only
forgiveness that makes any sense at all.

The girl awakes. She wants you inside her.
The two of you wash the night from your mouths
with slices of sour green mango.

228

Jogging with the Philosopher

for JoeVolpe

Descending into Valley Green is easy
because its all downhill. Gravity.
A delightful invention. Thanks to Newton,
I can take the time to notice squirrels,
the grace of trees, the blessing of wind,
sometimes even a deer with spotted fawns.
You can't beat that on a Sunday morning.

We can even talk on the way down,
though I have to admit that I
do most of the talking. The philosopher
isn't given to words. Once in awhile
he'll allude to Epictetus
or the perfect wisdom of breaking
the collarbones of graffiti artists,
a solution without the tyranny
of state-sanctioned death, but a lesson
not to be quickly forgotten.

Jogging along the creek is equally
pleasant. The water sings swiftly here
among the rocks, there pauses to reflect,
the ducks in every weather unperturbed,
as if they remember the soft scrunch
of our feet on the gravel path, as if
we were old and trusted companions.
I could jog for miles beside the creek
and we do, the philosopher
taciturn but not at all unfriendly.

It's coming back out of the valley
that always kills me. Gravity. That
dirtbag Newton. And the hill nearly
a mile long and practically vertical.
I do it just to remind myself
how truly miserable life can be.
Halfway up my lungs begin to burn
like I've swallowed fire, my legs become
like tree stumps, and my heart cries out,
"Oh, world! Oh, madness! God, oh, God!"

Right about then, the philosopher
slowly but surely accelerates.
I manage to gasp, "You bastard."
The philosopher only grins.

Cliches Become Cliches
Because They're True

for Ben in Friends Hospital

You have to understand the way things are:
fire lives in this man's dreams, the way it
roils across the land like water churning,
the way it scours flesh from living bones.

That one's fine and delicate as lace
my grandmother used to make on Sunday
afternoons when she was young and people
stayed at home on Sunday afternoons.

This one's got a wife and kids afraid
they'll let him out again too soon and he'll
come home a nightmare with the family name
and nothing else familiar but their fear.

The woman by the window slashed her wrists.
And that one near the door has got a child
she tried ten years to bear and now can't bear
to hear or see or even think about.

God only knows what breaks inside the brain,
or why. You have to understand the way
things are: there's only circumstance, and chance,
and there but for the grace of God go I.

Pabst Blue Ribbon Beer

Jeff and I were eight or nine the day
we snuck into the basement den,
opened a bottle of his father's beer.
What was this stuff his father drank?
How did it taste? Why did Dr. Apple
have a special room that seemed so full
of mystery? Mrs. Apple even drank
a Pabst Blue Ribbon now and then,
and she was everything I ever
dreamed a mother ought to be.

Jeff had it made: beautiful mom,
dependable dad. I never saw
them arguing, never heard them
raise their voices to their children.

Our basement didn't have a den.
Our basement was a dingy place
with crumbling walls and cobwebs clinging
to the pipes, and old wooden crates.

Jeff took a sip and made a face,
and then I took a sip and forty
years later I can still recall
the vile taste, so bitter, the confusion
of that moment: how could people
I'd have given anything to be
their child enjoy so foul a thing?

We poured the bottle down the sink,

never thinking that in five more years
Mrs. Apple would be diagnosed
with multiple sclerosis
that would slowly over thirty-five years
reduce her to a shriveled fetal ball
abandoned by her husband, left
to lie alone through all those years
to finally die alone in a room one
floor above where Jeff and I thought
nothing in the world could taste this bad.

A Meditation on Family Geography
and a Prayer for My Daughter

Seven generations of Ehrharts
are buried in Hampton, Pennsylvania,
but I never lived there.
My father left when he was young.

There are Contis buried in Gettysburg
where my mother grew up,
but she wasn't born there
and she, too, left when she was young.

My parents are buried where I grew up
in Perkasie, Pennsylvania,
but I wasn't born there
and I left when I was young.

I have a brother in Colorado.
I have a brother in Montana.
I have a brother in Thailand.
They have a brother in Philadelphia,
but it isn't my home. It's only
a city; I only live there.

My wife's mother is buried on Martha's Vineyard,
but she wasn't born there.
She never even lived there.
She was born in Fresno, California.

She's only buried on Martha's Vineyard
because my wife's father grew up there,
but he wasn't born there either
and he left when he was young.

His mother is buried next to his wife,
but his mother's house was sold long ago
and he likely won't be buried in Massachusetts;
he's married again and living in North Carolina.

Scattered across the globe we are,
the living and dead of our two families,
and the older I get the more I wish
for the comfort of generations,
for the solace of long acquaintance with place
and people around me who care.

The worst is when I think of our child
and what she'll have when her parents are gone:
relatives scattered across the globe,
most of them nothing but names.

Mostly, even with Leela and Anne,
I feel like a mariner lost at sea
or a small cry lost among the stars.
How will Leela feel when it's only her?

God grant her a loving and faithful mate.
God grant her loving and loyal kids.
God grant my daughter a place in the world
surrounded by people who care.

Detroit River Blues

I was jogging. It was cold.
I was wearing my hooded sweatshirt
and behind me for miles up Woodward
Avenue to Grand Circus and beyond
was a pastiche of retail shops and banks
and abandoned buildings boarded shut,
men and women in business suits
and street people and bums and the guy
in a wheelchair hawking the news:
"Scab newspapers not sold here!" he shouts—
big union town, Detroit, and a strike on.

Me, I'm living at the Downtown Y, nine
floors up and a window overlooking
rooftops and alleys and empty lots,
so I like to go jogging to clear my head,
take my mind off just how lonely I am.

But just as I get to the river,
the wind skipping across the water
like a good flat stone and smacking me
right in the face, the river all whitecaps,
a big damned ore boat, the *Walter J. Todd*,
comes plowing along on its way to who
knows where, and I think to myself
if I hijacked that ship I could
sail it up the St. Lawrence Seaway
to Newfoundland and then turn south
along the Atlantic coast to Cape May
and up the Delaware Estuary
all the way to Philadelphia.

236

I could dock the ship at Penn's Landing;
I could walk to where you work;
we could have lunch together.

I could be having lunch with you
instead of freezing my ass off
watching that boat disappear down
the river without me. Me without you
and the wind rising. And I think to myself
it's a hell of a day to go jogging.

About the Author

W. D. Ehrhart was born in 1948 in Roaring Spring, Pennsylvania, and grew up in Lewisburg and Perkasie, Pennsylvania. A US Marine Corps veteran of the Vietnam War, he has worked as a merchant seaman, laborer and journalist, among other occupations, and has been a writer-in-residence for the National Writer's Voice Project of the YMCA of the USA, Visiting Professor of War and Social Consequences at the University of Massachusetts at Boston and a research fellow in American Studies at the University of Wales, Swansea, UK. The recipient of Vietnam Veterans of America's Excellence in the Arts Award, the President's Medal from Veterans for Peace, a Pew Fellowship in the Arts for poetry and fellowships in both poetry and prose from the Pennsylvania Council on the Arts, he currently teaches English and history at the Haverford School in Haverford, Pennsylvania. He lives in Philadelphia, Pennsylvania, with his wife, Anne, and daughter, Leela.

Books by W. D. Ehrhart

<u>Poetry</u>
A Generation of Peace
The Samisdat Poems
To Those Who Have Gone Home Tired
The Outer Banks & Other Poems
Just for Laughs
The Distance We Travel
Beautiful Wreckage: New & Selected Poems

<u>Prose</u>
Vietnam-Perkasie: A Combat Marine Memoir
*Passing Time: Memoir of a Vietnam Veteran Against
    the War*
Busted: A Vietnam Veteran in Nixon's America
Going Back: An Ex-Marine Returns to Vietnam
In the Shadow of Vietnam: Essays 1977-1991
Ordinary Lives: Platoon 1005 & the Vietnam War
*The Madness of It All: Essays on War, Literature and
    American Life*

<u>As Editor</u>
Carrying the Darkness: The Poetry of the Vietnam War
Unaccustomed Mercy: Soldier-Poets of the Vietnam War

<u>As Co-editor</u>
Demilitarized Zones: Veterans After Vietnam (with Jan
    Barry)
Retrieving Bones: Stories & Poems of the Korean War
    (with Philip K. Jason)

239